Hunger into Health

Hunger into Health by Erik Talkin

♛|FOOD LIT PRESS

Cover and interior design: Felix Talkin / felixtalkin@gmail.com

Acknowledgments

Thanks to all Talkins and Jorgensens for love and inspiration to try to be healthy myself, rather than just preach it to others!

Thanks to my board chairs for advice and mentorship: Scott Coe, Frank Abatemarco, Melissa Petersen, George Thurlow, Barry Spector, and Vibeke Weiland.

Thanks to the fabulous staff members who I have worked with over the years. Their dedication to our mission is an inspiration. Especially Fred Smith, who passed recently and gave 26 years of his life to the Foodbank.

Thanks to all of our caring and visionary donors and supporters in the community. You are the ones who made it possible for us to do something new.

Erik Talkin
February 2018

Fred Smith's retirement party, July 2016. As the t-shirts said: 26 years serving the Foodbank, a lifetime of keeping it real.

Table of Contents

Educational notes

You Say Tomato…

A Note on Confusing Nomenclature

When this book mentions a "food bank" using two words, that refers to the generic type of food distribution organization. When "the Foodbank" is used, I mean our food bank — the Foodbank of Santa Barbara County. Don't ask me why our name is a single word; the reason is lost in the swirl of time.

While we are concerning ourselves with such niceties, let's clear up one endless confusion. A food bank is a large regional distribution center that provides food to member agencies (think wholesaler). These can include food pantries, who distribute to individual clients (think grocery store). These smaller organizations can sometimes call themselves food banks, which muddies the issue and drives normally sedate food bankers crazy.

Individual Donations
Retail Donations
Purchased Food
Food Drives
USDA Commodity Foods
Backyard Bounty Gleaning

Direct Service Programs
300 Partner Agencies
Mobile Farmers Markets
Senior Brown Bag
Healthy School Pantry

Hungry
Santa Barbara
County
residents

Foreword

I first met Erik when the Foodbank of Santa Barbara County honored my wife Susan at their Table of Life gala, for her long support of the Foodbank's Empty Bowls fundraiser. This is a great event that provides attendees with delicious soup from local restaurants and beautifully thrown bowls from local potters. What I like about it is that it's not the usual standing around with a glass of wine and an appetizer event. It goes straight to the mission of the Foodbank, which is to feed people and build community.

I've been advocating around this issue for decades because it's so basic to our ability to have a healthy community and a strong country. In my travels and by talking to many people, I've discovered that hunger can often be invisible. People don't like talking about it and they often don't like asking for help either. This means it can continue unchecked. Children are not able to concentrate in school, parents do without to ensure that their kids can eat, senior citizens barely scrape by.

What impressed me about the Foodbank, right here in my own backyard, was that not only do they help an incredible one in four people in Santa Barbara County, they also focus heavily on moving people out of food insecurity.

I spent time with Erik to learn more about his Foodbank's approach. Erik is a colorful local figure with an impressive collection of hats and that dry humor and British accent that he failed to completely shake after growing up there as an expat. He explained to me that the Foodbank believes that providing food alone is not enough. You have to pair it with building food literacy. This can be a parent's ability to stretch a dollar by planning and cooking healthy meals or a child's ability to both appreciate good food and actually want to go into a kitchen and make it. This education is vital to build life-long resiliency in the face of financial ups and downs.

The last few years I have been engaged as national spokesperson for Share Our Strength's *No Kid Hungry* campaign, not because I want to fight the good fight, but because I want to win it. Making all Americans hunger-free is more than possible, and the thought-provoking ideas (and actions) in this book sketch one possible road map for making it happen.

The approaches that Erik and his team have pioneered in Santa Barbara have been widely influential across the food bank and emergency food network — prioritizing nutrition; providing education as a first thought, not an afterthought; partnering with healthcare providers; working with a broad group of stakeholders in the local food economy through a local Food Action Plan — these are all major steps forward from what you and I probably understood to be the world of a food bank.

The journey of Erik's organization over these last ten years can be the journey of many of the other 64,000 non-profit agencies, large and small, spread across the nation, who try to solve the problem of hunger every day. It shows that we have an opportunity to move beyond providing groceries to offering the empowerment, education, and hope that everyone in America deserves.

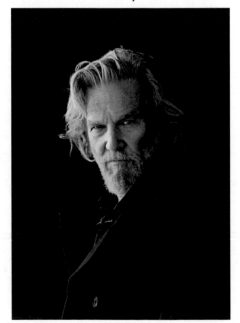

Jeff Bridges
Santa Barbara CA
2018

Introduction: The Challenge

I began this book while I was living on food stamps.
I had $6.23 a day to purchase enough food to eke out three
nutritious meals. My kitchen was comprised of a single gas burner
and one pot in which to work any culinary miracles.

By the time I reached Day 30, I was HUNGRY. For the last two
empty days, all I'd had to eat were three apples and a fistful of kitten
cookies. My stomach felt like it was at war with itself. I found it
hard to concentrate and was perpetually grumpy. Someone gave
me a T-shirt that said: *Sorry for what I said when I was Hangry.* (A
combination of hungry and angry). I think it was a hint.

On Day Thirty-One, a new world dawned for me. I got up and
cooked fresh eggs and spinach. I looked in the refrigerator and saw
provisions enough to make meals for the rest of week.
I felt secure — food secure.

One author, one challenge, one box of groceries.

What miracle occurred to
change my life situation
overnight? All that had
changed was that I had ended
my commitment to living on
food stamps for thirty days
as part of my biannual food
security challenge *(www.
foodsecuritychallenge.wordpress.
com)*. I didn't sign on for real
food stamps — I earn too
much — instead, I took the cash
equivalent of what people in my
area would get in benefits and
shopped for food with that.

I hope that the challenge is not seen as a stunt or an insult by people who have no choice but to live that way every month. It serves to remind me though, of what the people I work with have to go through. Gwyneth Paltrow made it 4 days before consciously uncoupling from a similar food security challenge. Cory Booker made it a week and now he's a senator. For me, it is a way of focusing my mind on why I am doing this job and what it can mean to those we work with.

For ten years, I have been CEO at the Foodbank of Santa Barbara County, which distributes ten million pounds of food a year across our county, both through our own education and distribution programs and via a network of 300 member agencies and programs.

This book represents the culmination of a decade spent trying to rewrite the rule book on how a food bank or any non-profit organization can approach the way it works with the community and how we can find lasting solutions to seemingly intractable challenges.

This book follows the parallel track of my story and the story of the Foodbank of Santa Barbara County's evolution to a new kind of non-profit. **Sidebars** provide additional information on people and situations that played a key part in the story. At the end of the book are some **Educational Notes**, advice for non-profit leaders on how to undertake, staff, and pay for the transformation of your organization. What are the painful lessons I have learned and how can they be applied?

Whether you come to this book as an individual or as a change maker within an organization, you will hear a story of transformation — of ourselves, our non-profit organizations, our communities and our country.

This transformation did something better than turning lead into gold. It turned hunger into health. Here's how it happened.

It's the Food, Stupid

Food is a necessity, like air and water, but unlike the other two, it has dimensions far beyond sustaining life. Food can be a pathway to physical health and increased self-respect. It can create opportunities for local businesses and community development. Alternatively, it can lead to obesity, food deserts, institutionalized malnutrition, and even addiction when processed junk food takes control of the pleasure centers of the brain.

The realization that you can do a lot more with food than feed people has nourished my imagination and career for the last seventeen years, during which time I have been solely involved with nutrition-based non-profits. I have discovered that providing food is a way to draw wary people into situations in which you can provide something more lasting than a full belly. You can use food as leverage to offer education, inspiration, and empowerment. The other thing I learned is that individual health and community economic health are always tied together and so can be used to improve each other.

This was not always my relationship to food.

I was a U.S. Navy brat, growing up from the age of four as an expat in England. My lieutenant commander father was assigned to Naval Intelligence at the Navy Headquarters building in London's West End. As an experiment, I was sent to a very proper English school. I had to wear a blazer and tie and eat

Brother, can you spare a dimple?

awful 1960s/70s British food. This included fish fingers, which we suspected were made with real fingers, and brussel sprouts that were so over-cooked, some of the more talented boys could use their tongues to extrude them through the gaps in their teeth.

At the end of the day, I would come home and eat American food from the PX (armed forces exchange store). This included frozen, processed comfort food and lots of soda and candy. Iceberg lettuce and bricks of frozen creamed spinach were what passed for healthy vegetables. Meanwhile, the Brits were eating jellied eels, rhubarb, and parsnips — things I was not getting involved with, whatever the benefits for international understanding.

Yet, even then, there was some spark of interest in food as something that could be more than fast, salty, and sweet. My dad had served time on submarines, including the USS Nautilus (the first submarine to travel under the polar ice cap), and during his service he had developed into a good cook. When you're stuck underwater for weeks with limited food supplies, you have to learn some culinary skills to prevent mutiny.

My dad's ability to make the best of whatever food was on hand would later prove very inspiring.

Another early childhood influence that would become central to my later work was a children's picture book, *Stone Soup,* in the version by Marcia Brown. I was inspired by the

Callow as they come.

simple brown and orange pictures and the intriguing tale of the three soldiers who demonstrate an interesting mix of community organizing and con-artistry by convincing the villagers that together they can create a feast out of nothing more than three round, heavy stones. This simple tale was to provide a lot of ideas for how a community could feed and build itself up.

Later, my early career as a playwright on the London Fringe and low-budget filmmaker ·provided me with skills that were to prove useful in forging and communicating a vision for a healthy community.

After attending University College London in Bloomsbury, and co-running The Mighty Pen Production company, I returned to the U.S. in 1998, with my then wife and three kids, on a mission to become a millionaire Hollywood scriptwriter. Despite an agent and a manager and a spec script optioned, the dream machine spat me out and I had to hustle to feed the family. We had moved to Santa Barbara in Southern California, not realizing that first you make your millions and *then* you move to Santa Barbara.

I became intrigued by the city's plethora of non-profit organizations. (With over 1000 non-profit organizations, Santa Barbara has one of the highest ratios per capita anywhere in the U.S.). In England, the state had looked after most social

Directing Helena Bonham Carter in my short film, "The Gallery".

service functions. Here in America, it was much more down to a patchwork quilt of financially-challenged non-profits to undertake that work.

After working at a large musical theater that ground itself into bankruptcy with an unmelodious crash, I worked at a non-profit called *City @ Peace*, which taught at-risk teens mediation and conflict resolution through drama. Even here, I was learning how important food is to achieving broader aims. Amongst the teens who the organization appealed to, our nickname was City @ Pizza because the kids knew there would be food and that was a big part of the draw.

Then I became Executive Director of an organization called the *Community Kitchen of Santa Barbara*, which operated out of the Casa Esperanza homeless shelter on Santa Barbara's east side. With a kitchen provided by flame-haired Santa Barbara philanthropist Lady Leslie Ridley Tree, we provided meals for those living in the shelter and a lunch program for the wider community.

It was quite a life lesson for me, seeing up close the challenges of homelessness. One day in the line, I saw an ex-investment banker and an ex-hitman standing next to each other in the lunch line having an animated conversation. Many were wrestling with addiction, or mental illnesses that they were self-medicating. I listened to the stories people told themselves about how their current situation had come about. I also realized that many more of us are a couple of paychecks away from drifting into that situation. Even more profoundly, I witnessed the response of people in the community to homelessness. They were confronted by a dark mirror of what their own lives might have been or could still be like. This vision engendered fear and revulsion in some, and the most beautiful love and compassion from others. Occasionally too

much compassion! Volunteers who served food on the line would sometimes ladle out huge trays of food, thinking the more food, the more love they were giving. I soon realized that too much food could be as much of a health challenge as too little.

And then one year, the Foodbank of Santa Barbara County, who provided our organization with much of our food, suddenly began to receive a large amount of extra fresh produce from all over California. Now we could get as much fresh fruit and vegetables as we could use. Within a matter of weeks, the transformation in the health of our clientele was staggering. A sweet local lady named Renée who came for lunch each day suffered from a long list of health complaints. Her complexion was always sallow to the point of greyness. Once her vegetable consumption increased dramatically, her skin began to bloom, first into beige and then a glorious pink!

When the job at the Foodbank opened up, I was intrigued. What if we could bring that kind of radical improvement in health not only to the transient residents of a homeless shelter, but to the whole of Santa Barbara County? What if we could reach children with good food and the skills to use it? What different paths would their lives take?

I wanted that job, and on April 15th, 2008, I walked through the warehouse doors of the Foodbank of Santa Barbara County as it's new CEO.

You Know, it's a Bank, Only with Food instead of Money

I like to think I landed this job because of my vision for the organization and my proven track record in fundraising, but I have to wonder. The future Board Chair (and no-nonsense Baltimore businessman) Barry Spector interviewed me for the job at a table outside Santa Barbara's Coffee Cat (RIP). He was wary at first. Who was this chancer with the hat and the British accent? But then we discovered we were both obsessive fans of the HBO series *The Wire.* After years of unsuccessfully trying to convince the rest of my family that this was the greatest TV show in history, finally someone understood! I wasn't sure how an encyclopedic knowledge of the cat and mouse of the Baltimore drug trade was going to help me run a non-profit in genteel Santa Barbara, but I got the job and began to discover what a food bank really was.

Our large Santa Maria facility serves as the hub for the county.

Food banks act as large storage and distribution centers that bring in many million pounds of food, both donated and purchased, from the surrounding area (and even out of state). They then store it safely before distributing it through a network of member agencies. Think of all those small non-profit organizations or youth or church groups who might cook or distribute food. They don't have the storage or cooler/freezer space to store large amounts of food. They don't have access to large quantities of free or near-free food. That's why they (and you) need your friendly area food bank.

We are a member of a national affiliate organization of 200 food banks covering every part of the USA, called *Feeding America*. It provides training and auditing of  our activities, grants, and national level advocacy. It also promotes cooperation between food banks, which learn from each other and purchase food cooperatively. It's a sweet arrangement, although trying to get 200 regional organizations to agree about anything makes cat herding seem therapeutic. CEOs of the organization have come and gone, but doing an incredible job of listening to and working with member food banks has been Feeding America President, Matt Knott.

In Santa Barbara, the Foodbank has large warehouses in the north and south of the county that serve the 300+ member agencies who come, sometimes every weekday, to pick up food for their programs. Our member agencies include food pantries, residential facilities, children's programs, and senior centers.

When I joined, food banks were acting as middle men, getting food to outside agencies and hoping those agencies would make the best use possible of it. The experienced food bank CEOs I met told me that nothing beyond moving food through the warehouses was our business. This also extended to asking questions about what kind of food we were receiving and distributing. It was all about

We provide food to over 300 local nonprofit agencies and programs.

volume. CEOs would brag about the poundage of their food banks, no matter how junky those pounds were. It didn't take long to realize that this kind of mass myopia created big health challenges for those they were trying to serve.

On the program front, our food bank did run a large number of mobile pantries to get food out to areas that didn't have non-profit programs, and we had a senior brown bag program providing groceries, but beyond that, we only had one other program. This was the Backpack Program, which provided a bag of food for a child from a low-income family to bring home on the weekend. I opened a bag and saw things like the Tijuana Mama Extra-Hot Sausage crammed full of nitrates, salt, and artificial hot sauce, not things growing bodies need.

Looking through the warehouse, I also saw the kind of food being donated that people wanted to get rid of: junk food, out of date food (which we toss) and a lot of leftover Christmas and Hanukkah items in January. Then there were the sheet cakes, candy, soda, and glow-in-the-dark cookies.

I asked one of the then board members about all the candy

and soda we were giving out. He sat me down and, I'll never forget, explained how the candy and treats were "a light in a dark tunnel for children with hard lives." I wanted to tell him that the light in the tunnel was the express train of poor health that was about to slam into them. However, having just joined the organization, I had to bite my tongue and bide my time. This was a wonderful non-profit doing great things, but I knew something had to change.

Sidebar: Hungry People in Santa Barbara? Ha ha ha!

Santa Barbara is known across the country for its ideal year-round climate and beautiful beaches, for its Spanish architecture, and for being home to stars like Ellen and Oprah. When I went to national conferences, people stared incredulously at me when I told them about the food insecurity in Santa Barbara County. *Are the poor people consigned to a diet of caviar and crackers?* burbled the think bubbles above their heads.

But as Roxy Music sang many eons ago: *In Every Dream Home a Heartache.* The uncomfortable truth is that only 11 out of 58 California counties have more hungry people than Santa Barbara. In ways large and small, we serve one in four people in our county. Our aid might be fresh fruit for kids attending low-income preschools or long term help for seniors, but it is still a startling statistic.

Food Insecurity: No Fun for All The Family.

I remember visiting Brazil a number of times as a young man, once to make a TV documentary, and in Rio de Janeiro, the poor people live in the favelas up in the hills. At night the favelas would light up with kerosene fires. In Santa Barbara, things are flipped and better-off people are living up in the hills.

Many who live on the edge of poverty work in the service and hospitality industries in the south of the county. In the north, there is poverty connected to seasonal agricultural work and lack of other major industries. This means that a lot of families regularly need help. The City of Lompoc, in mid-county, was assessed in 2013 as having a child poverty rate of 40%.

There was one other statistic that was less crushing and would work in our favor if we wanted to get healthier food to people. Santa Barbara is in the top 1% of agricultural producing counties in America. Wow! We have the green stuff here, even if 97% of it goes straight out of the county.

Taking these factors together meant we had considerable need here, but also an opportunity to utilize our abundant fresh produce as a key to making a greater change in people's lives. The question began to form in my mind. How could we get more healthy food, and how could we educate people to make use of it?

Hand Out or Hand Up : False Dichotomy

As I began to settle into the job and became aware of the many things I didn't know, I realized that it wasn't just the quality of the food we were giving out to people that there were issues with. The way in which we and our member agencies were interacting with people when we distributed that food was also a problem.

It was disempowering. People would stand in line in the hot sun, often for over an hour, to pick up a bag of groceries. This would fill bellies for a day and the Foodbank would "succeed" at its mission to get food out to people in need. There would be more poundage to brag about to the other food bank CEOs, but as I watched people walk away, I realized their lives had changed very little. We had done nothing to help ensure that they didn't need to come back tomorrow. We imagined that people's circumstances would change — that they would get higher paying jobs and no longer need our "emergency food". But that didn't seem to be the case.

What we were doing was providing charity and feeling good about what goodly people we were. Sometimes volunteers would get annoyed when they saw that some of the recipients of the food donations did not seem very grateful. I understood at least something of that response after seven years of working within a homeless shelter. While the people the Foodbank served were overwhelmingly not homeless, all people in situations of great stress look for strategies to maintain their self-respect. It may come across as rudeness to a volunteer, but generally it's not meant that way. Their pride is a coping mechanism that helps them keep going and deal with the next disappointment and the next, without falling to pieces. This is worth remembering the next time someone down on their luck doesn't immediately thank you for your kindness. They have much more on the line than you do.

Let's consider this notion of charity a little more, because it really is central to how these services are able to empower or disempower people. Consider how you respond to the following supposition:

Give once and you elicit appreciation;
Give twice and you create anticipation;
Give three times and you create expectation;
Give four times and it becomes entitlement;
Give five times and you establish dependency.

This idea is explored in Robert Lupton's book *Toxic Charity*. He says: "Food in our society is a chronic poverty need, not a life-threatening one. And when we respond to a chronic need as though it were a crisis, we can predict toxic results: dependency, deception, disempowerment."

Lupton's basic supposition is that a lot of what non-profits and churches do to assist people has a negative rather than a positive result. Ouch! He is not questioning people's motivations, but rather the unintended consequences of rightly motivated efforts. He believes that if "emergency" relief does not transition to other types of help in a timely manner, then compassion becomes toxic.

I think this is an important consideration for non-profits to keep in mind when they are analyzing what kind of services they offer people, but it is also only one strand of a complex situation. You need to feed the hungry person first, then quibble later.

Lupton largely ignores the systemic constraints on the person living at or near the poverty level. My experiences of working with many low-income people have taught me a lesson that I didn't necessarily want to learn: that all of the bootstrapping and chasing of the American Dream in the world cannot lift the majority of people out of poverty. Widespread minimum wage jobs, the practice of keeping employees at below 30 hours to deny them benefits, technological changes, and the things that people do to their bodies and relationships to cope with the grinding challenges of their struggle all conspire to keep people where they are. In the U.S. in 2018, you can work around the clock and still need help with groceries.

A key inspiration for me was the writing and work of Jan Poppendieck. Her book, *Sweet Charity? Emergency Food and the End of Entitlement,* was written in 1998. When I read it a decade later, it had a profound effect on me. It described the emergency mentality that I saw around me, as well as the head in the sand approach to the nutritional impact of the food that food banks had been providing and the need to find more sources of fresh produce within the network. Sue Sigler, the ED of the California Association of Food Banks, recently told me that she thought *Sweet Charity* was almost single-handedly responsible for bringing food banks into the public policy realm, which was an area considered best avoided prior to its publication. Jan has been active, both as an academic and also serves on the board of Why Hunger? in NYC. She has most recently written *Free for All: Fixing School Food in America.*

Needless to say, that volume is something of an eye-opener too.

With all these thoughts bouncing around in my head, I still figured there had to be a way to both provide food and relate to people in a manner that would empower, not disempower them. It would take a world-shaking event to make this clear to me. That event transpired in 2008.

Sidebar: Walking Talking Statistics

People often ask me, who is the typical person that the Foodbank serves? "Is it that homeless man with the Jack Russell terrier on a string, who doggedly hits me up for cash on the corner? Or is it that loud middle-aged woman with the ratty sun visor I see illegally cutting up newspapers at the library, and who seems to think the world owes her a living?"

I reply with a few simple numbers. As regards homeless people, only about 4-5% of those we serve meet this criteria. The figures most worth remembering are that an incredible 40% of those we serve are children under 18, while 25% are seniors.

As to the typical recipient of Foodbank services, if I look at combined statistics, it is a hardworking family of four with at least one family member in full time work. They want to provide for their children's futures while improving their current situation. But they don't earn enough to build up the savings needed to cushion them from the catastrophe that can strike with any unexpected expense. Sometimes they need our help, sometimes they don't.

Would you like to meet some people instead of some statistics?

Walk with me down Stern's Wharf on one of those perfect Santa Barbara 70 degree days, and you will see hundreds of families out enjoying the sea air and an ice cream or watching amateur fishermen catching nothing more than a little peace and quiet. Here comes one particularly close-knit family, Daniel and Maricruz Salazar, and their children Eileen, (7) and Daniel Jr (5). Following them, while trying to not to slip between the planks, is Holiday, their pet chihuahua.

Daniel and Maricruz have been married nine years. Daniel is a house painter and works two and a half jobs to try and help his family make it. He ensures that his kids work hard at school, hoping they can have more opportunities through better education. Unfortunately, like millions of other working families, the Salazars teeter on the brink of financial meltdown every month.

Eileen is a smart, lively girl. When she finishes her homework, she often watches at the window for her dad to come home, knowing he will be gone before she wakes in the morning. She's hoping for some small time they can spend together, despite his exhaustion.

Eileen says that "she's glad they can get healthy food from the Foodbank, because she wants her dad to work harder and faster and be home sooner."

We all know a balance has been lost in our society, and it hurts everyone on either side of the scales. If you're on the side that is dipping down, the challenge is the world you're struggling with right now, but even if you are on the elevated side of the scales, you are facing questions about what type of world is being handed to your children and grandchildren to live in.

Finding that balance again is work for all of us to do, for Eileen and for all our kids.

Interesting Times and the Caper of the Decade

"Never let a good crisis go to waste."
Winston Churchill

"May you live in interesting times."
Traditional Chinese curse

The recession of 2008 had a profound effect on the emergency food world. Organizations that focused on helping those in short-term need because of economic dislocation suddenly found themselves overwhelmed by the numbers of people who needed assistance.

At the Foodbank, our own numbers shot up by 35% at the same time as the traditional avenues of bulk food donation were drying up. Continued efficiencies in the grocery supply chain now meant less food for food banks, as did the explosion of dollar stores which became secondary markets for off-brand food that had often been donated to food banks in the past.

However, because of the generosity of people across the country, cash flowed into food banks and emergency food organizations. Locally, the Santa Barbara Foundation provided a generous extra grant and, as is often the case, those in the community who could least afford to give, gave the most. We brought in as much food as we

could get our hands on.

Yet, this was also a moment of opportunity for a better future. If every penny we received was spent on food that would soon be consumed and gone, we would be leaving everything else unchanged. We needed to invest in a longer-term vision of people and their lives. We were sick of being the band aid; we wanted to be the cure.

We could have carried on as the heroes of the day and taken on a crisis mindset of "just getting through." Instead, we resolved to put aside a modest 10% of non-donor-directed funds we were receiving to save for strategies that would help give people better food and provide education to help them make better use of it. At the time, I probably would have been drummed out of my job if this strategy had been common knowledge. In the hysteria of the crisis, it would have been seen as heretical and selfish.

We also didn't suspect that the crisis would turn into the new normal and that the recovery, when it came, would be at the expense of jobs and enough hours on those jobs to support a family. Still, once the worst of the initial recession had subsided, it did give us the opening we needed to act. JFK may have got his characters mixed up when he said that the Chinese for crisis was also the same as that for opportunity, but we were going to make the best of the "interesting times" we were living through.

When I talk about how the FBSBC morphed from being a traditional food bank to one that wanted to bring about a much more active and urgent transformation to people's lives and a change to the food system, I talk about it in terms of a caper, or a heist. A thrilling tale of how a mild mannered non-profit organization decided it wouldn't take it anymore, went rogue, and pivoted to undertake the real work it knew needed to get done. Of course, we went rogue in the nicest way possible. But eggs were still smashed to cook up this particular nutrient dense omelet, and those eggs were both inside and outside the Foodbank.

The idea of the pivot is commonplace in the tech world. You make something and then when things are not exactly working out, you need to think of new real world applications for the underlying proprietary technology that you have come up with. Often where you end up is far from where you started. At first Pinterest was a home shopping app; Twitter was initially a side project for a podcast listing service; and Nokia started off in the 19th century as a wood pulp mill before transitioning eventually to phone handsets. Now they have sold that business, one in which they were once dominant, to Microsoft, and are pivoting again.

Non-profits do not find it so easy to pivot.

They are typically operating in a well-established niche that they are afraid of losing should they shift focus. They fear that moving in a new direction means that donors will abandon them and they will have to shutter their doors. This is not a wholly unreasonable fear. Many non-profits have chased new and highly competitive sources of funding and shifted what they were doing, for the simple reason that this was where the money was. This type of behavior leads to mission drift. And if no one is quite sure what you do, then they're never quite sure why they should fund you rather than another organization.

A pivot is not "following the money," it is a much more considered move. Also, experience suggested that if we leveraged our food distribution machine for another purpose — to draw people into education and empowerment training that boosted their self-sufficiency — then this was a crucial service, not provided elsewhere.

But how could we get there from here? Did we have the hip moves to pivot?

An encouraging note from a staff member in the middle of our pivot.

In the case of the Foodbank, I had to deal with some deeply challenging internal cultural issues. When I joined the Foodbank, it was very much a "family business" in that the Operations Director

As the wildflowers danced in the wind, things seemed so peaceful from the outside.

oversaw both north and south county warehouses. That person's partner worked in the North County warehouse, supposedly reporting to the then warehouse manager, who was an ineffectual manager and yes man. In the South County warehouse, the same Ops Director's niece was in charge of our relationships with member agencies. This allowed one person to exert an unhealthy level of control over a large part of the organization. This person was certainly a hard-working, dedicated employee, but saw their way as the only right way, and was dead set on the idea that the Foodbank should not evolve forward from being a simple food-in, food-out warehouse. This person also played the two warehouses against each other, so as to maintain undisputed control. It took a while to unjam the situation, and ultimately, a new Operations Director, Jamie Nichols, took over to begin the healing. Jamie used his own leadership vision to make both warehouses one functioning body — with occasionally differing practices — but keeping one common goal. This was to prove crucial in being able to move the organization forward. As well as Jamie's contribution, we had the total commitment and fundraising drive of Jane Lindsey, who served as our Director of Development for nearly a decade. Along with the dedication and hard work of Carrie Wanek as CFO, these three members of the leadership team allowed the organization to be both secure and ready for growth.

Once we could move forward without every little change within the organization being a battle, we began to introduce program and nutrition changes.

Internally we were transforming, and what we were doing externally was changing, but guess what? It wasn't enough. The community's perception of who we were as an organization needed to change, so that they would support the evolution of our mission.

Unfortunately, there was a lot of work to do in that department as people's view of the Foodbank was stuck in the 1980s. If I went up to someone in the street (and I did) to ask them what images and

ideas came up in their head when they thought of food banks — they would describe food pantries, food drives with barrels at stores, a turkey donation, and the idea that we are much busier at Christmas than at other times of the year. Yes, we are busier at Christmas, only because that is when people are reminded that we exist! People are consistently hungry year-round.

Prior to our pivot, we were seen as an essential organization for the community, but one whose job was to tamp down a problem that could never be fixed. We wouldn't accept that and were determined to find that fix.

But before we could do that, we had to face up to some ugly truths about what we had been doing and discover the true meaning of good food.

Sidebar: The King of Food Insecurity

Primary Drivers of Food Insecurity

UNEMPLOYMENT

POVERTY

LOW ASSETS

Food Insecurity

Hunger is a word understood by all. It evokes a visceral response, a physical feeling that we have all experienced. What about the phrase "food insecurity"? Not so much, right? It sounds like some wonkish technical term. Yet it is probably one of the defining terms for American life since the 2008 depression. One definition of food insecurity is: *not having*

ON AN EMPTY STOMACH, I CAN'T ~~laugh~~ Learn

FEEDING AMERICA

enough healthful food available at all times for all family members to live active healthy lives. Sounds pretty basic for the land of plenty. Waves of amber grain from sea to shining sea, right? The truth is that one in six Americans struggle with food security. Six and a half million of those people are children. Even for many working families the problem becomes particularly acute toward the end of the month. All the money has already been spent on rent and medical bills and transportation. The family budget item that gets squeezed is the only easy variable — good food. This creates a negative cycle whereby bad food makes people less healthy and less able to work and, consequently, less able to afford good food. Many people, even in households with at least one full time worker, rely on donations from pantries supplied by the food bank network.

The challenge that food banks and other emergency food providers face is the institutionalization of their services. It is now very common for people to work low wage, low hour jobs with poor benefits, and they are becoming increasingly reliant on food bank food to maintain what they are coming to consider as the new normal of food security in their lives. Food banks were never designed for this purpose.

Food insecurity has a profound effect on children. Scientists have identified toxic shock effects on the young growing brain that can lead to both physical and psychological impairments, which can ripple out over a lifetime. There are many factors that cause people's relationship with food to go out of balance:

• *scarcity at a young age,*
• *feelings of low self-esteem caused by not being able to currently provide for the complete nutritional needs of a family,*
• *body and health image issues resulting from family and societal pressures,*
• *lack of other ways to deal with stress and emotional issues, and lack of empowerment around nutrition and health.*

Find that hard to believe? Then consider a man who is probably the number one candidate for the patron saint of food insecure Americans, Elvis Aaron Presley. His future health was clearly shaped by early experiences of hunger. Squirrel and other roadkill were items on the Presley dinner menu. The gospel elements of his vocal style can be traced to the fact that as a young boy, he was brought to many churches in the South because of the fried chicken dinner offered to congregants after the service. Basic psychology tells us that if something is denied us, we want it more. And so, food became an obsession with Elvis, and as he became more successful and money for food was no longer the issue, the need to binge eat became more and more pronounced. A particular favorite of Elvis' was the Fool's Gold Sandwich, weighing in at 6000 calories.

Fool's Gold sandwich or alien autopsy, you decide

This infernal combination of a pound of bacon, a jar each of peanut butter and grape jelly, and a whole loaf of bread. Elvis would have six of them made at a restaurant in Denver that specialized in them and then fly in by private jet with his entourage and consume them in the airport hangar washed down with champagne. There is actually a great book looking at Elvis' life through the lens of food, called *The Life and Cuisine of Elvis Presley.*

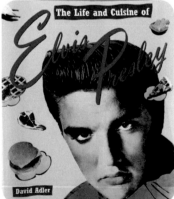

Elvis found it impossible to escape from that formative relationship with food. Many of us have emotional triggers that cause us to eat mindlessly and to excess — imagine how they are multiplied if your body and psyche have real experience of doing without food. This is very common in food insecure people who get stuck in a cycle of eating too much when food is available' because they are fearful over the times that food has not been freely available.

Lovely Leptin and Ghastly Ghrelin

Now that the Foodbank was becoming better funded, it was time to move forward on the issue that had been unsettling me since I first walked in the door — the food.

In terms of food quality, food banks had been getting a free pass for decades. They could shrug their shoulders and say they were just distributing whatever food distributors/manufacturers donated to them. The food was free and people shouldn't whine about the Christmas candy in July or the *Blue Pepsi*. Remember that?

We didn't feel blue, but the Pepsi marketing department did.

It came and went in the blink of an eye and food banks received an ocean of the soda that America scorned.

It's a truism that any business is only as good as the quality of its product. Most non-profits provide a service instead of a product, yet a food bank is very much about the product. I was sick of being embarrassed by the contents of some of our warehouses and having to steer people away from the junk when they toured the Foodbank. And so, in 2010, we made it official policy to no longer distribute candy and soda.

It was a controversial move at the time. Luckily, the board member who had sung the joys of candy had moved on, as he didn't like the direction the organization was moving. Yet, there were still concerns that agencies, donors, and individuals would be up in arms about having their freedom of choice to choose junk being undemocratically ripped from them. My belief was that this choice always remained. Candy and soda are the cheapest and most readily available food-like items in America. It was the good stuff that was not so easily had. *That* was the missing choice for so many people.

We didn't want a food bank made of candy.

To my surprise and delight, the tidal wave of outrage against us being high-handed nutrition zealots never materialized. Our market research on individuals and agencies demonstrated that people were desperate for as much healthy food as they could get. We did lose some donors, such as a local soda distributor, who refused to let us have surplus water unless we also took their surplus soda.

Tragically, a lot of the candy ended up in landfills, while the soda was poured down the drain and the bottles recycled. My belief is that it's a greater desecration to shove this junk into the stomach of a food insecure child than it is to bury it deep in the earth. It's great to have some candy now and then, but we are working with families who often have had their health compromised by too little nutrient dense food and who have been filling the emptiness with junk for years.

This stand against junk (and we where one of the very first food banks in the entire network of 200 national food banks to take such a stand) allowed us to begin to put our own house in order and build the credibility to move forward with other plans to transform the nature of how we engaged with the community.

Yet, I was in for a painful discovery. There were nutritional problems that getting rid of candy and soda weren't going to solve — and they were problems food banks had helped to create. Excuse me?

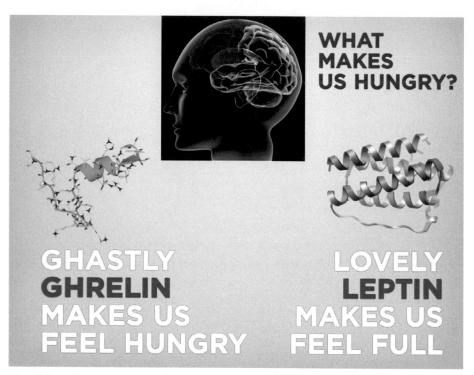

WHAT MAKES US HUNGRY?

GHASTLY **GHRELIN** MAKES US FEEL HUNGRY

LOVELY **LEPTIN** MAKES US FEEL FULL

Food banks are on the frontline of the battle against hunger. It is our sworn enemy and we will never surrender (insert any additional war metaphors you are partial to). What if food banks were inadvertently doing things to *increase* hunger as well as eradicate it? Noooo!

I made this painful discovery in 2012, soon after hiring the Foodbank's first registered dietician, Serena Fuller, Ph.D. At that point it was a rarity for a food bank to employ a dietician. Many organizations, if they were interested in investing in this area at all, were happy with a nutritionist, whose job was to supervise any nutrition education programs, as well as to fume helplessly at some of the more horrific stuff lying in wait on the shelves of their food bank.

Serena was brought on as our Health Education and Evaluation Manager. She had a background in obesity research and public health. Her remit was to improve the quality of our food, but also to develop an evaluation framework that would enable us to prove that providing healthier food to people had better long-term outcomes relating to health. You'd think that was a no brainer, but it would turn out to be challenging to prove clinically.

Hippocrates made a good point in 470 BC, and it resonates increasingly over the last few years. Food is medicine and medicine food.

It became clear that we were giving a lot of bad medicine with the good. I learned about brain chemicals like ghrelin (which makes us feel hungry) and leptin (which tells us we are full). When I examined the typical food that a food bank had on its shelves, I discovered that much of the food increased supplies of "ghastly ghrelin" to the brain and suppressed "lovely leptin." This double whammy was made worse when I learned about the insulin spikes that so many sugary foods caused. These created energy crashes and perversely made people even hungrier than when they started.

This was a situation that we needed to find a pathway out of. One solution was to purchase only food that was nutrient dense. The Foodbank spends hundreds of thousands of dollars every year purchasing items such as proteins, pulses, and grains that are harder to get donated in the quantities needed. If we made sure these items were low salt and had no added sugar, that was a good start.

The other solution was to focus more heavily on all the fresh produce that we are able to get our hands on. Not only do we have a lot of produce locally, we are also able to take advantage of purchasing a range of produce for pennies on the dollar from our membership in the California Association of Food Bank's Farm2Family program. Through this program, we collectively hire food solicitors throughout California that negotiate both the donation and purchase of "seconds" from California farmers. In a world that seeks surface perfection, these seconds are the

California
ASSOCIATION OF
Food
Banks

heads of broccoli that are too small, or the strawberries that are not plump enough. Or the "ugly" fruit that is still perfectly useable and healthful. They are shipped in refrigerated trucks and distributed efficiently to the network of member food banks.

Feeding America began to respond to this situation on a national level. Michelle Berger Marshall, the organization's Managing Director of Community Health and Nutrition, worked hard to push the nutrition agenda, and to encourage food banks to realize that they couldn't just use fresh produce as a fig leaf to cover over all the other highly processed, sugar-and salt-laden food they were distributing. The concept of 'Foods to Encourage' was developed, based on the USDA's My Plate template, setting out what foods should be emphasized to both member agencies and individuals. The next challenge for us in Santa Barbara, with our fresh produce focus, was to get people — especially kids — to want to eat all this green, hard, mud-encrusted stuff.

FEEDING
AMERICA

FOODS TO ENCOURAGE

- **Fruits and Vegetables** *Fresh, frozen, canned, dried*
- **Whole grains**
- **Low-fat/Non-fat dairy**
  Skim, low-fat, dairy alternatives
- **Lean proteins**
  lean meats, poultry, seafood, eggs, legumes and   seeds/nuts
- **Water**
  Plain water

<u>Second level of emphasis</u>
Thresholds/Cut-off points for
- Trans-fats
- Saturated fats
- Sodium
- Added sugars

**Note ALL thresholds will be in line with existing federal nutrition program guidelines when available (i.e. CACFP, WIC etc.) **

Feeding the Future

What is this fear of vegetables many of us had as children? I have already opened up about my painful childhood experiences with creamed spinach. For many youngsters, part of the issue is that vegetables are not inherently sweet or salty, which are the desires that our palates are steered into developing from an early age. Yet I also believe it is connected to the way in which vegetables are presented

to children. *"Eat two more mouthfuls of your cabbage, and then you can have your dessert."* Vegetables become at best something that has to be got through, so you can move on to the "good stuff."

What if we could get to children's palates *before* sweet and salty are all they want? And what if we could involve the children, putting them in charge of creating vegetable dishes they would want to eat? When I looked around, I couldn't find any programs that combined food distribution and food education, and so we set about creating them.

Previously, nutrition education was a largely theoretical offshoot of human biology. It was about chemicals and nutrients, and for the non-science kids like me, that wasn't going to work. We developed a sequential series of food literacy programs for children, designed to deliver them up into adulthood with the skills needed to be healthy with food. And we called it **Feed the Future**. And they were so inspiring, I went crazy designing all the program logos.

Our educational work begins at the preschool level with the **Food Literacy In Preschool (FLIP)** program, where community volunteers trained by the Foodbank go out to preschool programs to teach young children about the taste, touch, and smell of a variety of fresh fruits and vegetables. This is done by having the child sample a simple recipe they help make utilizing the item, then following this with a game or song or book about the produce item. Finally they are given a small bag of the produce to bring home and share with their family.

Volunteers Ann and Mike teach at our Carpinteria Kids' Farmers' Market.

This approach is carried forward at our **Kids' Farmers' Market (KFM)** which is a more advanced version for grade school children attending schools that have a high percentage of free and reduced lunch students. We set up our own farmers market with stalls of fresh fruits and vegetables from the Foodbank. Children get to pick a more substantial produce bag to bring home with them. They then receive an interactive cooking lesson from a volunteer educator, in how to

turn all this alien produce into a delicious meal

that they would like to eat. The minute children are involved in making something with the vegetables, they take on the ownership and confidence to enjoy produce items they would have rejected only minutes ago. The kids then go home that afternoon with both the food and the knowledge of what to do with it. This is a powerful combination that has had profound results for many families. Children cannot control the food intake of their families but they can be strong influencers. We were thrilled when the program was singled out for national recognition as the Best Child Nutrition Program of 2011 by Feeding America.

The next progression in our cycle is the **Teens Love Cooking Program (TLC)**. This is the real deal, an eight-session cooking course that introduces children to a range of simple culinary concepts. It is often the first time that children have been trusted with knives in the kitchen or allowed to do more than

TEENS LOVE COOKING

inserting something into the microwave. The program ends with a fiesta, where the children cook a meal for their families, who come to the school. This final step validates their efforts in the real world and allows them to transition their skills to the kitchen at home. We had a local County Supervisor who visited the program and was extremely reluctant to sample what the kids were cooking, which on that day was beet pancakes. He'd never wanted to eat beets as a child and decided that they must still be nasty. Rather than risk losing a few votes, he did finally decide to try a mouthful, and loved them. The beets were subtly incorporated into the recipe to build its nutritional value and he hardly noticed them, despite the reddish-pink nature of the pancakes.

The famous beet pancakes.

All of the Feed the Future programs adhere to our three-part criteria for programs:

1. They provide short-term hunger relief with healthy food;

2. They provide food literacy (cooking, shopping, nutrition) training to help people make better use of food to stay healthy; 3. They can be run by trained volunteers.

In this way, the Foodbank becomes a tool with which the community takes responsibility for solving its nutritional challenges.

Hunger and lack of food is a huge problem, but so is the inability to use food effectively. Other countries with lower average per capita amounts of disposable income have far lower levels of food insecurity because people there are better able to make nutritious meals with what ingredients they have at hand. These skills have been lost to many today and it is vital that we help people reclaim them.

Other food banks now run a range of nutritional programs, and a number have adopted our programs, but there still remains an education gap. Given the increased emphasis on fresh produce to fill the hunger gap of missing meals for food insecure Americans, this demands a commensurate increase in the focus on the education that will allow people to want to cook more produce. Unless we do this, we might as well toss all this new produce away in the dumpster and save our clients the trouble.

Local foundations, like Hutton Parker, led by Tom Parker and Pam Lewis, understood the need for education as a means of securing long-term change and supported our early efforts. In 2011, we developed a way to ensure that this food literacy and education was made available to whole families. It was a chance to build a whole new type of relationship with traditional "clients" and it was called the Healthy School Pantry.

FOODBANK FLIP

Food Literacy In Preschool

1. Food preferences are decided by preschool. Our community volunteers are there to introduce fresh produce through tasting games and activities. And there's even a bag of produce for the family.

FOODBANK
SANTA BARBARA COUNTY

This is how we will

feed the future

bring about the rise of food literacy and the end of childhood hunger in a single generation

NUTRITIONAL INDEPENDENCE

6. This is where we put it all together! We make sure our young adults can budget, shop and cook for a lifetime of nutritional independence.

PICNIC IN THE PARK

Free Healthy Lunch for Kids!
Gratis: un almuerzo saludable para los niños!

5. Kids are often hungry in the summer with no free school meals. Their brains and bodies still need to keep growing, so volunteers prepare and serve healthy lunches and provide games and food literacy training.

Kid's Farmers Market

FOODBANK

Mercado de Niños Granjeros

2. We bring a farmers' market to low-income afterschool programs, providing fresh produce for the children as well as a cooking lesson into how to make all those icky vegetables delicious. They go home with both food and skills, which can begin powerful family transformation.

Your Healthy School Pantry

3. Local schools become a focus for ending hunger and celebrating health and good nutrition. The whole family is involved in improving their food literacy and food security.

Teens Love Cooking

4. Real teens, real knives, real cooking. An intensive cooking course ending in a Fiesta cooked by the students for their families.

SIDEBAR: FOOD LITERACY

In 1961, the year of my birth, Cuba organized a national literacy campaign that mobilized more than a million Cubans as teachers or students. In that same year, 707,000 Cubans learned how to read, raising the national literacy rate to 96%.

It is commonly appreciated that if you are illiterate or innumerate, you go through life with one hand tied behind your back. It is my belief that if you are "food illiterate," you face a similar challenge. You can't cook healthy meals yourself, and so are at the mercy of highly processed, pre-packaged, or fast food. We have all witnessed a food illiterate teenager open a refrigerator packed full of ingredients and say "There's nothing to eat in the house."

FOODBANK
SANTA BARBARA COUNTY

FOOD LITERACY

Proficiency in food-related knowledge and skills so I can take charge of my own nutritional health

My Healthy Plate

1/4 Starch

1/2 Vegetables

1/4 Protein

1. BUDGETING
How much can I spend on spend on food? How can I use it best?

2. PLANNING
No one has time to write a menu for every meal, but I can make sure I have the basic ingredients for enough meals.

3. SHOPPING
How do I avoid expensive convenience and make every dollar count to keep healthy?

4. COOKING
What meals are healthy, tasty and quick after a long day at work? How can I keep it fun?

5. STORING
How can I cook extra and store it so I don't have to cook every day? And how can I rotate those extra meals to keep things interesting?

My Healthy Plate from the Institute for Family Health

There are many definitions of food literacy. My definition is proficiency in food-related skills and knowledge. That includes the following skills:

Budgeting and planning - What money can I get together for food, and what are the best ingredients for me or my family to make the most nutritious meals possible?

Shopping - Where can I find the bargains and the freshest stuff? How do I avoid coming out of a store having spent all my money and holding a bunch of junk that will be gone in a day?

Cooking - Where the rubber chicken meets the road. How do I get the skills to whip out simple, delicious dishes without spending my life in the kitchen? Especially if I really don't even have much of a kitchen.

Storage - How do I find the storage options to allow me to cook a week full of meals in one day, so I don't feel I'm endlessly eating the same meal?

Once you have these skills, you have a lifetime of health available to you through the joy of food. You can save a lot of money and teach your children the same life skills that will free them from a life sentence of ramen and burgers. It also gives you the skills to get through times of having little money for food while still remaining healthy.

My daughter Mia was only four, but with clipboard in hand she was doing a nutrition class with a group of adult diabetics and still had fun.

My oldest three adult kids (Ella, Felix, and Lili) all eat pretty healthily (heck, they're Californians now) and Mia, the six-year-old, (who slipped into the lineup somehow) started learning kitchen knife skills with her own pink-handled paring knife at the age of four (to her mother's occasional perturbation).

Natalie Orfalea demonstrating a certain food literacy.

Orfalea Foundation and Food Literacy

In Santa Barbara, we were lucky to have the Orfalea Foundation, change-makers in the area of food systems and school food. Natalie Orfalea is a thought leader in this area and an inspiration to me and to food banks to up our game and always to play for the long term. The foundation focused on discharging its funds over a compressed time so that they could initiate real change in food systems work. Before they sunsetted, they were able to provide some seed funding for the Santa Barbara County Food Action Plan (of which more later). They still maintain an excellent website (www.orfaleafoundation.org), which contains information about the lessons they learned, so that they can continue to be a resource in this vital area.

Starting a New Conversation

Food literacy is the foundation of the Healthy School Pantry. This concept came about in the wake of a disturbing trip I made to a local school that was the recipient of a traditional food bank school distribution via the "Backpack" program. This provided bags of food for kids to bring home for the weekend. The bags were put in a room and all the other kids knew that the poor kids were the ones who went into that room and came out with a bag. I could see the humiliation on those kids' faces. It was disempowering and it put too much responsibility on the child to be responsible for the food needs of the family. Backpacks are warranted in situations where there is an unstable home life, but counselors can identify these students and food can be dispensed in a subtler manner. We had to be able to do better.

I had also begun to realize that unless people were in the middle of a major natural disaster, or their physical or mental circumstances meant they were unable to look after themselves, the provision of emergency food ultimately made little difference to their long-term nutritional or financial health.

However, if you paired this food with food literacy skills, people became more independent and creative when it came to making a dollar stretch to create their own healthy meals. It empowered people to get involved in their own decisions around being healthy with food. How could we fan these sparks of empowerment? How could we make our friends and neighbors in the community more like partners in a shared mission to help each other be healthy, instead of the recipients of charity?

As somewhat of a punk rocker in my youth, I have rarely been known as much of a hippie, yet I found myself thinking about this issue in terms of energy flow. The traditional way that food banks and other emergency food organizations operated was very much a one-way transfer of energy. *We are the charitable ones, and we are giving to you, the recipient of charity.* Also, as far as volunteer involvement in these programs went, volunteers would come in, help, then leave again. If I've learned anything, it's that long-term change only comes from long-term involvement. But how do you keep involved in the long-term without building the types of dependency I mentioned earlier?

To address this dilemma, a model called community engagement began to seem most appropriate. The definition of this for me — donning my hippie beads for a moment — is a back and forth exchange of energy, work, and ideas that creates a circle of mutual and equal benefit within a community.

The Foodbank could begin this process with a question as simple as: *"How can we all be healthier?"* That's because this is a question anyone can have a valid personal response to. Whether you are a billionaire or a beach bum, you have opinions on how you can maintain your health. The conversation becomes an equal dialogue around a shared interest. Yes, there is vast inequality in the provision of expensive medical care to fight disease. But there does not have to be so much inequality when it comes to preventative approaches to avoiding those diseases in the first place. Simple exercise, stress reduction techniques, and eating enough healthy food are options available to many of us.

The community engagement model ensures that those with expert knowledge or with resources can add to the discussion, but that their voices aren't allowed to dominate or to de-skill the community they are trying to help. Instead, the community is empowered and supported to help itself. Volunteers come from the micro-community being served and remain within it.

We wanted to try and create a program that experimented with these ideas in a way that wouldn't jerk people around and would show us quickly what worked and what didn't.

So, come join us at the Healthy Community Pantry (HCP). If you flew your personal drone over one of Foodbank of Santa Barbara County's Healthy Community Pantries you would get a sense of a circular energy flow in action, as people move through the different actions and activities, both receiving and giving of themselves.

HCPs began as Healthy School Pantries. These take place in the *"after-after-school space"* in a school hall or community center. This is the time when families are picking up kids from their afterschool activities.

As always, the initial draw is the food, but this is not just random food that the Foodbank needs to get rid of so it can keep cycling through its warehouse stock. Amongst other food, we have the menu ingredients that are required to make a specific recipe. As you enter the HCP, you get to taste that meal, and then a volunteer shows you how to make it, which typically involves at least one novel item. We grow lots of persimmons in Santa Barbara, for example, and do you know five things to make with persimmons? No, I didn't either.

Attendees pick up a "passport" which requires them to shuttle through some educational or health screening stations before they pick up the food for the meal they just learned how to prepare (plus other food). The passport approach is a gentle way of steering new people to take the risk of trying out the interactive educational elements. These stations might include:

- **Instruction on growing some of your own food with some free seeds or a plant from a volunteer representing our *Grow Your Own Way* program;**
- **Education on cutting out soda consumption with the Rethink your Drink curriculum;**
- **Diabetes, hepatitis, or dental screenings; and/or**
- **Cal Fresh (food stamps) sign up;**

Zooming back up to our drone-eyed view, we can see the energy moving around the room as community members share information and approaches to good health.

Our own evaluations showed that we were on to a good thing. People really responded to the friendly community atmosphere. Health was not a prescription, it was friends and laughter and connection over good food. These were principles that would stay with all future programs.

We were thrilled when we were awarded our second Hunger's Hope Award from Feeding America and the *Healthy School Pantry* was acknowledged as the most innovative children's nutrition program in the food bank network.

We felt we were achieving something significant in a grassroots way. But how could we prove that what we were doing was increasing food security? What was our theory of change?

SIDEBAR: BIKE BLENDER

What use does a food bank have for a bicycle? It isn't refrigerated; it can't carry ten pallets of food. In fact, it's mounted on a stand and won't get you anywhere, no matter how hard you pedal. Yet it does have one useful feature, because mounted on the back is a blender powered by the pedals.

We deploy the bike blender to make healthy smoothies at a range of public events promoting the Foodbank, as well as at some of our children's programs, such as Picnic in the Park or Healthy School Pantry. Kids climb on and pedal the blender, creating smoothie magic. The bike blender is the perfect

As usual, the CEO "managing" the labors of others!

demonstration of our message of good food plus exercise equals health.

At a public event, we could give someone a flyer about our hunger into health message, or we could ask people to experience it, via the bike blender. We make our famous kale smoothie, which contains frozen fruit and juice with the invisible presence of the wonder vegetable, and just like with our other programs, kids love to consume what they have been responsible for making.

Too often, a food bank's display at a public event features a food drive barrel and someone with a clip board, collecting volunteer sign-ups. The bike blender acts as a huge draw at a wide range of events. Climb on and start peddling!

FOODBANK
SANTA BARBARA COUNTY

SHreK SHaKe

Prep time: 5 mins
Servings: 4

Serving size: 1 Cup
Tastes: 8

Ingredients

1¹ᐟ² Cups frozen unsweetened pineapple chunks
1¹ᐟ² Cups100% pineapple juice
¹ᐟ² Cup low-fat vanilla yogurt
2   Cups loosely packed fresh kale

The Theory of Change

After doing this job for a number of years, I realized that food banks across the country were providing a sustained level of food support way beyond what had been originally intended. When food banking first began, the goal was simply to distribute excess food and thereby avoid food waste. Now, the numbers needing our services had shot up because of the 2008 recession and they stayed up. It was as if we were doctors responding to a chronic long-term maintenance disease with a never-ending series of emergency treatments. Any doctor will tell you that this approach can keep the patient alive, but it is unlikely to promote recovery.

Food insecurity was becoming systemic, built into the standard flow of life for low-wage earners. I remember asking Marlene, an under-employed mother of three if she felt food secure, and she said: "Yes, because I can go to (Pantry A) on this day and (Pantry B) the other day." We had become part of many people's regular food landscape. The food bank network could not afford to be an eternal safety net that allowed employers to pay non-subsistence wages or to cap hours at a level that avoids benefits. There is a clear financial cost to these actions, and that cost was being shifted onto the food bank network and other areas of the safety net.

Our Brown Bag program helps keep seniors healthy and independent.

I began to consider a theory of change (the detailed measurable steps that could be contained in a logic model) that would allow food banks to work their way out of the "eternal crisis" situation that had been foisted on us. The need for this became more acute when fundraising softened, as donors perceived that the recession was over. We were assisted by long-term support from the Weingart Foundation and their local representative, Emilie Neumann, who saw the direction we wanted to move in and supported our journey there.

My belief was that our food bank needed to think, operate, and eventually be funded like a preventative health care organization, much like the wellness department of a local hospital works to keep people healthy so they don't need more expensive medical services. In the same way, we could be the wellness organization for nutritional health. We didn't need a billion dollar miracle drug, we could raise people's health in the cheapest way possible through what they eat.

Our range of 'preventative' programs could provide the food literacy skills that would allow people to be healthier. Yes, many might still need food help from time to time, but building nutritional skills and independence would break the automatic dependence.

We want to present lack of access to adequate healthy food and

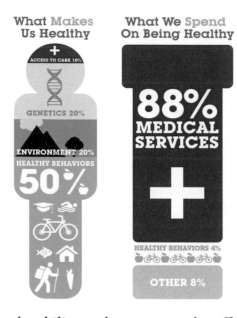

What Makes Us Healthy

ACCESS TO CARE 10%
GENETICS 20%
ENVIRONMENT 20%
HEALTHY BEHAVIORS 50%

What We Spend On Being Healthy

88% MEDICAL SERVICES

HEALTHY BEHAVIORS 4%

OTHER 8%

the skills to make use of it as an issue of unacceptable public health, which should be addressed, treated, and funded in that fashion. This is a gradual process, but I believe the food bank and emergency food networks remain the sleeping giants of the public health world. We can be the engine of the largest improvement in health since indoor plumbing.

To do this, the food bank network needs to have the ability to demonstrate the efficacy of our nutritional and educational interventions using acceptable public health criteria. Evaluation is the key to opening the door to a new approach and new funding from the Feds, from health insurers, and from donors who want to see a major long-term return on their social investment. And so, evaluation became a major focus for both our dietician and impact department. We began to utilize a widely accepted public health evaluation tool called RE-AIM (Reach, Effectiveness, Adoption, Implementation, and Maintenance). RE-AIM has been used nationally to assess a broad range of community health interventions from actions to prevent child abuse through evaluations of the efficacy of specific exercise programs for the elderly.

RE-AIM hypothesizes that the overall social-change impact of an intervention is a function of all five RE-AIM dimensions not simply the client-based outcomes. The implication is that to have a substantial impact at the population level, an intervention must do reasonably well on all or most RE-AIM dimensions, so that we know we are reaching the right people in an effective and sustainable manner.

One day soon, I believe that funding for organizations like ours will weigh the social impact returns we can bring against the financial investment made. We will have to make our cost benefit pitch presenting what improvements in health we will bring. We will have to show the specific groups we will touch and what specific disease areas we will help to mitigate or eradicate. We will need to demonstrate how much money we can save the city, county, and state in healthcare costs.

If we can put forward a persuasive argument, we will receive funding with the remit to deliver on our proposals. Our food and education programs and our demonstrated ability to link to a continuum of community support and empowerment for under-resourced individuals and families will help us make a strong case.

Utilizing this preventative approach and promoting it as a public health issue represents the broad strokes of a theory of change that will enable us to keep our emergency work for those who are truly in an emergency situation. It will also allow us to work with people in a new way and find a new way to give leadership in this area back to the community we serve.

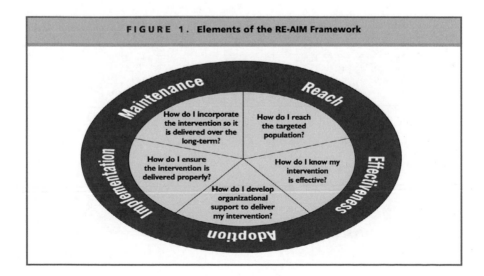

FIGURE 1. Elements of the RE-AIM Framework

Community Leadership: A New Pathway

Our new types of programs and approach required a total rethink of how we worked with people, both employees and members of the community. As much as Hippie Erik would have loved a spontaneous burst of energy to inspire the community to instantly organize its own education and programming, it was clear that it would take time for an approach like this to catch on. In the interim, we needed a way to draw the community into helping us run our programs. If we only provided programs that we had the staff to run, we would only be able to reach a tiny number of people.

Non-profit organizations typically start off as wholly volunteer groups coming together around a table to plot a community response to a social problem or a social opportunity (in the case of food banks, how to repurpose excess food).

Mia makes her way to the Foodbank's monthly Family Day, organized by the Mansbach family to introduce kids early to volunteerism.

Assuming the non-profit does
not pass away in its scrawny
infancy, it goes through a
gradual upward spiral of
increasing professionalism. It
finds a way to build a machine
for the long-term. That machine
is typically comprised of an
increasing number of paid staff.

This skyward cycle may result
in volunteers who become
something of an appendage, or
a phantom limb that takes on
the shape of the purpose it used
to have, but is no longer vital
to the continued health of the
organization. Instead, volunteers
become a way of connecting the

Heroic Foodbank volunteer. When they give you lemons...

community to the organization it supports; An interim stage to a
cash donation. This is a real shame, because people love to give of
themselves in what they do, and money can only say so much.

At the Foodbank, we had a mixture of long-term volunteers, who
were almost quasi-employees doing some warehouse, senior
grocery programs, and sorting jobs, as well as one-off volunteers
and groups who wanted to do something physical in the warehouse.
We were also lucky to have a super fundraising volunteer, the
amazing young man Jacob Mansbach, who started raising
thousands of dollars for the Foodbank by running triathlons when
he was eight years old! Along with his brother Joseph and parents
Jen and Mike, he has now raised over $80,000 for the Foodbank
through his Join Jacob campaign. It truly is a family affair, as they
run our monthly family day as well, a day when local families can
introduce their kids to helping others. In earlier days we had a lack
of this level of help, as well as very few knowledge philanthropists –

The Mighty Mansbachs – Jacob, Jen, Mike, and Joseph.

people who could lend their specific career expertise to our work.

We needed a new approach that was scalable and sustainable. And the only way to do that was to let the community into our organization in a whole new way — I am talking about the use of "community leaders" or "skills-based" volunteers. These are people who want to do more than de-stress over a huge bin of gently rotting carrot nubs. They want to make an impact on the community and the organization. They have ideas about how to do things better and they want the opportunity to be able to communicate those ideas. Our embrace of this approach has helped bring our food bank back to the community we serve, building long-term sustainability and forcing us all to improve our game and our outreach skills.

We now have community leaders who help agencies pick up food, drive trucks to pick up food, teach our educational programs, help with our accounts department, help with our marketing and events — the list goes on and on. Of course, there is always still a large need for regular volunteers, but what I am talking about are "super volunteers" overseeing other volunteers or knowledge philanthropists that might run a short-term task force or provide special knowledge.

Effectively integrating unpaid volunteers alongside paid staff is not straightforward. It takes work and training. We had training from an outside consultant (Vantage Point Consulting, experts in this field who are based in Canada). This training was provided to a wide group of managers. We also developed materials, like simple sample contracts stating what is expected of both parties, yet the reality was that unless we could find a way to evolve our culture to accept and integrate this kind of outside help, then this approach would have been doomed to eventual demise.

The book *The Abundant Not for Profit* features a chapter devoted to a case study on the Foodbank's work with community leaders, and how we have tried to share the execution of our mission with the members of the community. Even five years later, I am not aware of any other food bank in America that runs an ambitious program

WHAT ARE YOUR PERCEPTIONS?

VOLUNTEER

COMMUNITY LEADER

• *'Less than' an employee.*
• *Cannot be expected to always be reliable or accountable.*
• *Volunteers can't be fired easily, only scared away!*
• *Unpaid.*
• *No real authority / autonomy within the organization.*

• *Equal but different to an employee.*
• *Has signed agreement with joint expectations that both sides must meet.*
• *Community leader can be 'relieved' or reassigned.*
• *Paid - just not with money.*
• *Real responsibility and a voice in both role area and the organization.*

The **Abundant Not-for-Profit**

How talent (not money) will transform your organization

WRITTEN BY Colleen Kelly & Lynda Gerty

& THE TEAM AT
vantage point

department based on non-professionals both teaching and running programs.

The fundamental cultural fear we had to deal with in integrating a larger number of community leaders was concern amongst existing staff that they might lose their jobs. The assumption was that getting lots of skilled volunteers and training them would prove to be just a sneaky precursor to staff cuts.

This wasn't true. No one had their job taken by a volunteer. However, it made it clear that we needed to encourage a certain kind of employee — one with leadership potential. If staff could be open to finding ways of involving and managing volunteer staff, they would create an incredible value, and all but ensure a long and successful career at the Foodbank.

People's response to this was: *"How can everyone be leaders?* Who's going to do all the darn work!!" The way it works is for everyone to be responsible for leading and working with others from the community who want to connect with our organization. As CEO, I work with our Board of Trustees, who are the perfect example of community leaders who are committed to working for the organization, but who need guidance and support.

Leadership doesn't mean making speeches or bossing people around. It means being committed to moving the organization forward and developing your own skills and those of your team members. It also means a new awareness of ourselves as leaders in our community, representing and drawing people to the Foodbank so that we can achieve much more than we could have done by ourselves.

It is a wonderful opportunity for everyone to be a leader, whether you are a warehouse assistant leading a team of volunteers repacking bulk dried black beans into family-sized bags or a senior manager with a bunch of knowledge philanthropists helping you flesh out areas of your strategic plan. This is an approach that can ebb and flow within an organization, depending on the staff you are working with. I know that we will never arrive at a point of perfect integration between staff and community volunteers and leaders. It is always a work in progress, and we have had to embrace the joyful imperfection.

I did use one other approach to ensure that staff integrated use of community leaders, and that was to give them so much work to do, the only way they could achieve it all was to bring in help from the community!

Now that our award-winning programs were increasingly being run by community leaders, we could turn to an even greater challenge, how to involve our clients themselves in teaching and running these courses, so as to empower them within their own communities.

YOU MAKE IT HAPPEN.
YOU CAN END HUNGER.
Last year, volunteers provided 411 hours of food literacy trainings and 378 nutrition classes at our health programs. More information at www.foodbanksbc.org/volunteer

By the People, For the People

When you reach out and start a new conversation, as we did with the Healthy Community Pantries, it creates an opening to co-create something new together from within this more equal relationship. One creative possibility can be for people's interest and involvement in nutritional health to grow beyond their own families and extend to their friends and neighbors in the community. One avenue for this progression that we co-created, to work with Latina women in particular, is the Nutrition Advocates program.

Luz, a young mother in the Santa Maria area, came up as one of our leaders through this program. Her family lived on an incredibly tight budget, and if one of her kids got sick or the car needed a repair, it had a crippling impact on the family's ability to provide steady amounts of healthy food. She had utilized our services in the past and was amazed at how our approach had changed over the previous few years. She came for the food, but left with new knowledge, new contacts, and new resources. She had fun. She

wondered how she might get more involved in learning more about good nutrition both for her family and her friends within the community.

Luz became involved in our Nutrition Advocates (NAs) program. These geographically-based groups meet together with an organizer once a month at a simple potluck. When the groups start, it is with small group discussion and the initial focus is on trust

Lus Enriquez, Foodbank Nutrition Advocate.

building. We ask how to improve the Foodbank's programs to best meet the needs of the surrounding community, a place they are the experts on. The group then assesses opportunities for improvement and collectively comes up with solutions to support identified opportunities. Examples include the best time for a food distribution, how to spread the word about the distribution, and what types of foods are most useful.

Once the NAs see how their efforts have the power to change the Foodbank's services, they are then encouraged to take other steps toward nutrition advocacy and health equity. They receive training in nutrition, leadership, and community organizing. They then identify a community development project they would like to work on, which may be food-linked (such as improving school meals) or not (such as pressing for neighborhood improvements).

A group of our NAs in Santa Maria had a great success with this latter approach. The women had no experience in preparing and making a public presentation on an issue, but they did research and presented to the City Council on the need for and benefits of a traffic calming element in their neighborhood. Not only was the project approved, it created a powerful feeling of empowerment in women who had previously felt marginalized and unheard.

Nutrition Advocates are a model for basic advocacy that can expand beyond the confines of simple food distributions, with individuals working towards projects that promote health and food security in the broader community. Each group of NAs has unique needs with different desires to organize around things such as community garden development, using food stamps at local Farmers Markets, healthy school breakfasts, and lunches or grocery store access. Food banks provide the meeting place, training, and resources, and the NAs provide the local knowledge and the passion to improve their environments. This collaboration is a powerful tool for change.

The program was supported in its early days by forward-looking local philanthropist Sara Miller McCune, through her foundation that has focused so effectively on local social change work. This grassroots approach allows the Foodbank to act as a catalyst to encourage micro-communities to take ownership of their own nutritional health and that of their friends and neighbors. Some NA groups work better than others, some fall apart, some are too busy or really want to connect instead of saving the world. Each of those results is fine, because the network of connections that grow to strengthen community health invariably benefits in ways visible and invisible.

Maybe a simple potluck can be the beginning of an amazing transformation for a community!

Once you learn yourself, it's fun to teach others.

Sidebar: The Hunger into Health Blog

It was clear that to get enough support for what we were trying to do, we would have to spread these ideas and practices further, and so in April of 2012 I made the first post on my blog, Hunger into Health.

The blog was originally written for my peers in the food banking world. I wanted to put out ideas and solicit them. At the time, there was not a groundswell of sympathetic interest for these kinds of notions in the food banking world. (Remember, the first three priorities drilled into me were: 1. Pounds, 2. Pounds, and 3. Pounds).

I kind of loved this, being the punk rebel who was swimming against the stream. I remember the first Feeding America national conference after I launched the blog. I snuck into the conference room early in the morning while the tech staff were on a coffee break. Keeping careful watch, I slipped from table to table putting out flyers to promote the blog. By the time the conference staff noticed my tasteless breaking of accepted norms in distributing outside materials, it was too late and everyone was seated. I was also lucky enough that one of my heroes in the food banking movement, Matt Habbash, CEO of Mid Ohio Foodbank, had picked up a copy of the flyer and made reference to it in his remarks from the podium, saying that this was exactly the kind of health focus that could

Matt Habash, CEO Mid Ohio Foodbank.

spur a needed new direction for food banking.

Gaining some early credibility was a huge help to me in getting people to openly consider the ideas I was promoting. It also served as something of a rallying point for the other people in the network who were interested in new approaches. I was originally aiming to influence CEOs, but soon discovered that the blog was keenly read by those at more junior levels who were desperate for a change in their food bank's approach to both food and programming.

I stuck with a style that was broadly humorous and relied on flippantly-captioned photographs to illustrate points that were being made. In a world of painfully earnest non-profit blogs, it began to get some traction and to be read beyond the Feeding America network, by smaller agencies with big ideas and by researchers and individuals with a passion for this area. Clearly a lot of people were frustrated with our lack of success in shortening the line of those who needed our services. How could we begin to meet to come up with new ideas about ending hunger?

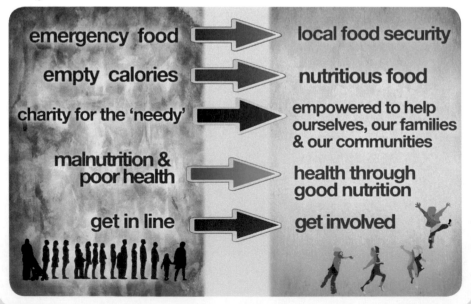

It Takes a Nation of Villages

One of the most interesting and challenging parts of my job is the constant need to move from a micro to a helicopter view of the world I'm involved with. You can't get more small scale than sitting in a group of half a dozen Nutrition Advocates trying to figure out what we can do to fix the local food system, and you can't get much larger than sitting with hundreds of your peers nationwide to wrestle with the same problems.

Feeding America has national gatherings for its member food banks. The California Association of Food Banks has its own meetings and trainings too. I have worked through these existing national structures to get the word out about our approach in Santa Barbara. Over the last decade, I have spent three years on the National Advisory Council (NAC) for Feeding America and served six years on the board of directors of the California Association. There is also another grouping that I have found useful for identifying conspirators who want to upset the apple cart of the conventional emergency food world. This is a group that comes together to explore, test, and execute sustainable food security strategies and seeks to build a national movement to enact systemic change.

The worst thing about it is its name: *Closing the Hunger Gap.*

Closing the Hunger Gap 2017: From Charity to Solidarity

It started off innocently enough as a conference, and how earth-shattering can a conference be? I attended the first one, in

September 2013 in Tucson, put on by the Community Food Bank of Southern Arizona, and was blown away. I had no idea there were so many amazing ideas and amazing people struggling to put them into action. The idea of "closing the hunger gap" was intended to focus on new ways to build food security, but it was so much more than that. People were taking innovative approaches to food justice, farm to table, food hubs, and on and on. From the Community Food Bank, Robert Ojeda and Leona Davis became key inspirational figures for me. They weren't "in charge" of their food bank, but this didn't stop them from doing everything they could to steer it in a more productive and forward-looking direction. I had found my people.

At that point in 2013, we were the "wild-hearted outsiders." These kinds of programmatic approaches were still viewed with some suspicion. In the past, food banks often treated any activity that was not distribution-based as window dressing; something bright and shiny for the pickier funders who don't love trucks. They were treated with unease within food banks because their outputs were harder to measure than pounds. However, by the third

biannual conference, "Charity to Solidarity," in Tacoma Washington in 2017, there were well over 500 attendees and it was much more like a gathering of the clans. Things were happening, and those things were speeding up.

I was asked to make some opening remarks at the latest conference, and posed a series of simple questions:

"Do you envision a time when nutritious food is recognized as a human right? When there is a political will to end hunger and its root causes? Do you envision yourselves as part of a growing, national network of collaborators and learners that engage with and support movements led by the people most impacted by hunger and poverty? Yes? Okay, you are in the right place.

Normally people have really boring conversations at conferences, about their missed flight connections, the food, even the headache-inducing pattern on the carpet. Thankfully, I'm with hundreds of people who I don't need to make small talk with. We can talk big, because we think big and whatever the size of our organization, we act big. We want to bring much needed transformation to our communities, using a tool as simple as food."

Both Closing the Hunger Gap and the world have come an enormous distance since the first conference. The world we operate in is finally waking up to the realization that the old ways of assisting people can perpetuate food insecurity. We are learning from our mistakes and learning from the communities we work with.

Out of the conference has come a movement that tries to keep the energy going between conferences and build a more inclusive and representative grouping. The non-profit *Why Hunger?* originally started by the singer, Harry Chapin (and now led by Noreen Springstead), has stepped in as the fiscal sponsor of the organization, and every month we do the difficult work of building that movement. Join us!

WhyHunger

Can We End Hunger in America?

Is this the $64,000 question? If only it came that cheap. Unfortunately, a Bread for the World Hunger Report estimated that in 2014, the health care costs alone of food insecurity in the U.S. were $160 billion. That's a lot of money. Working at a food bank in the United States in the early 21st century is a pretty steady gig. We do not appear likely to go out of business any time soon. And that bugs me.

Food insecurity is a pretty simple problem to solve. When put against so many other intractable problems we face, it seems almost laughably simple. Yet it hasn't ended and shows no sign of ending in the near future. Why is that? Of course, there will always be people who lose their job or can't get a job or hold a job. Then there are children and seniors. We know these needs will never go away, but they are manageable. The main challenge is the huge group of working poor who struggle to keep away from the poverty line, knowing that some modest misfortune could catapult them over the edge.

Part of the challenge is that we are coming at the problem from two directions. One is the provision of food stamp benefits (SNAP) and the other is the provision of emergency food through the food bank network and their 60,000 member agencies nationwide. SNAP benefits could be increased and made more freely available (because they have succeeded in at least preventing serious malnutrition from becoming pervasive in the U.S.). However, that is politically unlikely. In America, the prevailing philosophy is that we do not like to make it easy to be poor. The thinking is that if we can shame/motivate people to work harder, they will somehow bootstrap themselves out of poverty and the problem will be solved. That is certainly true for some people, but the ways the gears of our society crunch together, there will always be great numbers of people too crushed to do that. They will remain at or near the poverty line.

As I described earlier, in reference to people's visceral reaction to the homeless, there is a real fear of poverty in America. It's just not a personal fear of sinking into financial ruin ourselves, it is also that the problem seems so complex and overwhelming that we decide to focus on ameliorating the symptoms of the condition instead of trying to tackle the whole problem. ("We can't solve poverty, but we can push out more food.")

That has certainly been the history of the emergency food system. On the national level, we are very much stuck in the maintenance business rather than the transformation business.

I believe that we have taken the first steps toward transformation here in Santa Barbara, by seeking to turn hunger into a public health issue. Imagine if, on the national level, we pivoted to focusing on the issue of hunger as one of public health, and national food security organizations such as Feeding America, Share Our Strength, Bread for the World and others made the commitment to marshaling our combined efforts to raise the baseline health of Americans in the simplest and most cost-effective way possible — by raising the standard of their nutrition. It would be a historic game changer.

It would also have the power to bring in the Department of Health and Human Services as an additional funding partner. To make such a focus at the federal agency level requires these organizations to collaborate in a far more significant way than before, and to be ready to use a national drive for nutritional literacy and health as the pump-primer for next stage activities, such as community development and job creation centered around food.

We provide the most basic need possible — food. That doesn't mean we have to leave the potential for huge positive change in people's lives on the table and walk away. We can leverage that basic food need, and the access it affords into people's lives, to help them get ahead.

We need to reframe the issue from a negative one of charity for "the needy" to a positive engagement with people to ensure long-lasting nutritional health and have this seen as a vital and attainable public health goal. You may call me a dreamer, but as the song goes, I'm not the only one.

Sidebar: Jeff Bridges, National Hunger Activist

Santa Barbara resident and Oscar-winning actor Jeff Bridges — like thousands of others — is a long-term supporter of our Foodbank. But for decades, he has also been a vocal and effective anti-hunger activist. He is the national spokesperson for Share Our Strength's No Kid Hungry Campaign, and was an eloquent interviewee in the 2012 documentary, *A Place at the Table*. This film was a powerful look at the 49 million Americans who do not know where their next meal is coming from. It introduced us to people like Rosie, a grade-schooler in rural Colorado whose family of seven, because its income exceeds the annual limit of $28,000 per family of four, doesn't qualify for food stamps. Rosie's mother, who waitresses, can't afford vegetables for her family. Her teacher doesn't understand why she is so listless in class until she realizes Rosie is often hungry. It becomes apparent that gaunt bones and loose skin are not the physical attributes of hunger in America, where cheap carbohydrates lead to obesity. Many of the other interviewees find it difficult to talk about the issue. A Colorado policeman,

The Dude meets the Dudes and Dudess at the SB Warehouse.

whose job can't fully support him, struggles to describe his experience procuring necessities at a food pantry.

"We don't fund our Department of Defense through charity," Bridges says in the movie. "If another country was doing this to our kids, we'd be at war."

A few words with Jeff Bridges:

Jeff was honored at the Foodbank's 2017 Table of Life Gala for his activism against hunger, and recently visited our south county warehouse and spent time meeting with warehouse staff.

Jeff: I was very proud to receive this honor. I've received a few awards as an actor, but this really warms my heart, to be involved in a community where so many people want to help others. There is huge wealth but also challenging poverty, and that's why it's great to be in partnership with your organization.

Erik: *How did you first connect with this issue?*

Jeff: In 1996, my brother Beau starred in a movie (that I also had a part in) called *Hidden in America* about a family that struggles with food insecurity and where the father is too proud to seek help. It ended with the tagline: "On any given night, up to 5 million children in America go to bed hungry. How many of us will wake up in the morning and think about solutions?" That really struck a chord with me. I'd already been involved in the End Hunger Network and that only strengthened my resolve.

Erik: *What would you say is a major challenge in ending hunger in America? Because here in Santa Barbara County, the Foodbank is providing food in ways small or large to one in four people who live here.*

Jeff: People can have a resistance to hunger relief because they think that you will make people dependent on "hand outs" — even though your food bank's innovative programs are all about empowering people to be self-sufficient as much as possible. But ending childhood hunger is vital.

Erik: *They call children "dependents" for a good reason.*

Jeff: Exactly! And in my experience, people don't want to be dependent. They want to be independent, but for me, the truth is, we're interdependent. The only thing that holds hunger in place is a lack of community. Here in Santa Barbara County, we have a strong sense of community. You've helped create initiatives, like the Food Action Plan, that are all about long term solutions. I love the creativity of that work! And I think the motto of your organization, Hunger into Health, is such a great one, because it really is a simple health problem that we know how to fix. I also like to look at it as an issue of patriotism. I can't think of a more patriotic thing than making sure that everyone's kids — the future of our country — are healthy.

The Food Action Plan

Over the last few years, people have certainly viewed the Foodbank differently — and that has allowed us the space to take an evolved approach to our work. But we still needed to build a bigger shared perspective within the community that would allow us to grapple with the big food and health issues in our county.

This is not Silicon Valley. Wedged between mountains and the sea, Santa Barbara is not a place that attracts large new companies. But agriculture is one of the biggest economic drivers in the county, with $1.8 billion/year in crop production. When you factor in labor and other expenditures, it's a $2.8 billion/year industry for Santa Barbara County. We had to be able to leverage that, but how?

Other areas had food policy councils. These were groups of stakeholders from many sectors of the food system in a particular geographic area, often a city or a county. The idea is to have

participants representing every stage of the food system's great circle of life: production, consumption, processing, distribution, and waste recycling. Other Food Policy Councils ran the gamut from being well meaning talking shops to focused groupings that came up with the kind of joint projects that were of particular interest to us: building food security and health and creating new business opportunities relating to food. I knew I wanted the model that favored action over talk.

The Foodbank tried to provide financial support to a nascent effort at launching a local food policy council, but it never took off, because it was viewed as an elitist effort by south county progressives trying to enforce their own view of the agricultural world on the large growers in the north of the county.

We backed away for a while, but it was an idea that wouldn't go away. We needed a partner to get this thing off the ground. It had to be an organization that would be interested in food systems, only from a different perspective, so that we could both bring unique approaches to the table. But as the old song by Ian Dury states, *"trust is a must."* How could I find someone who would really want to see this through, and didn't just want to showboat or pick up a little extra foundation cash? I wasn't going to find someone like that by cold calling local non-profit leaders.

Fortunately, we have a non-profit in Santa Barbara called Leading From Within, led by Carrie Randolph, which is designed to help non-profit leaders renew themselves and break out of the scarcity/competition/isolation mindset. In its inception, LFW was very much the brainchild of Ken Saxon, a man who is an almost supernatural-level local force for good. The original iteration of LFW was a year-long retreat program called Courage to Lead. This allowed us to interact with our peers in a deeper, more trusting way. The sessions, co-run with Kim Stokely at the La Casa de

COURAGE TO LEAD

CTL Overview

CTL Highlights

COURAGE TO LEAD: PROVIDING LEADERSHIP TRAINING, NURTURING AND RENEWAL FOR NONPROFIT EXECUTIVE LEADERS.

Community Environmental Council

Maria center in Santa Barbara, were a wonderful experience. I loved the retreats: writing poetry, being in nature, trawling through past emotional baggage by utilizing listening circles based on the work of Parker Palmer. But, ever the multitasker, I was also on the look-out for a co-conspirator, someone who could help make the dream of a food policy group in Santa Barbara a reality. So, in April of 2013, I reached out to another Courage to Lead graduate, the (soon to be) CEO of Community Environmental Council, Sigrid Wright, and asked to meet.

Perhaps it was not a rendezvous of cosmic import to the degree of McCartney and Lennon hearing each other play at the Woolton Parish Church Garden Fete or Steve Jobs and The Woz meeting under the garage door opener in Sunnyvale, but it was still a significant moment in the evolution of the food systems work in Santa Barbara. The Community Environmental Council seemed like an unlikely partner at first. They were a respected organization with a long history of working for climate change solutions — solar, driving less, etc. Food banks were historically meat and potatoes types of organizations that were about delivering results today (preferably in a big

Sigrid Wright, CEO, Community Environmental Council.

Sharyn Main, Senior Director of Community Investment, Santa Barbara Foundation.

polluting truck), not protecting tomorrow.

And yet, there was something irresistible about these two divergent entities finding common cause in wanting to work to build a food system that would not only keep people healthy and financially thriving, but which would be sustainable and do minimum harm to the environment. The fact that I felt I knew and could trust her on a deeper level through our shared work at Courage to Lead gave us a much firmer foundation on which to build a partnership. The fact that she was super smart and had a grasp of detail that put my more visionary ramblings to shame didn't hurt either!

Our little cabal needed partners and funding to be able to move out of the "great idea" phase. That fall, we were able to interest two forward-looking partners, the Orfalea Foundation (whose food system work was detailed earlier) and our local community foundation, the Santa Barbara Foundation. Within the Santa Barbara Foundation (led by Ron Gallo), Sharyn Main was responsible for steering the LEAF (Landscapes Ecosystems Agriculture and Food Systems) initiative. This was a natural fit with our work. Sharyn's deep local knowledge of the food system and the environment, as well as her unerring skill at finding funding for projects from between the cushions of every metaphorical couch in the SB Foundation were a huge asset in getting things off the ground. From the Orfalea Foundation, President Lois Mitchell and disaster relief guru Barbara Andersen were early supporters, and when later the Orfalea foundation discharged all its funds, Barbara

LEAF INITIATIVE

LANDSCAPES ECOSYSTEMS AGRICULTURE FOODSYSTEMS

became our project manager on what soon became known as the Santa Barbara County Food Action Plan.

I liked the idea of a Food Action Plan - it sounded dynamic, like we were going to achieve things. Over the next two years we worked on the creation of the plan. The first stage was to put together an advisory board that would draw from all stakeholder areas. Our goal was to learn from the mistakes of the previous attempt to initiate a food policy council, by drawing together a broad and balanced group of stakeholders, and focusing on achievable goals that these groups could work on together. The unstated idea was that building new relationships amongst groups that rarely if ever communicated would bring its own reward over time.

Our advisory group of twenty-six was headed up by two county Supervisors, Salud Carbajal (now Congressman), a Democrat, and Steve Lavignino, a Republican, representing parts of the north and east of Santa Maria, which are heavily agricultural. These two already had a good working relationship. Maybe their parents had brought them up correctly, because they didn't automatically reject ideas that came from another political party. That sounds almost quaint as I write this in 2018!

Once we had our advisory board, we conducted stakeholder interviews, held bilingual community listening sessions up and down the county, and began to discover what was and wasn't working with the county's food system. We found out how this "system" impacts people, the economy, and the environment. We began to ask how those impacts could be made more positive.

It became logical to sort this feedback and our subsequent work into five key pillar areas:

- **Health and Nutrition**
- **Food Access and Justice**
- **Environment and Natural Resources**
- **Agricultural Viability**
- **Economic Development**

Past experience had suggested that there was no shortage of people with great ideas, but they would often rather keep their idea pure rather than cooperate with others to see what could be achieved together. This time, in order to make people's key interest areas practicable, we set up working groups for each of the pillar areas. We had 104 working group members who labored to turn vague ideas into workable goals. The intention was also to use this process to build out the networks, relationships, and broader community buy-in to make implementation possible. Foodbank board members like Narded Eguiluz and Wayne Elias, as well as staff, were heavily involved in this process, and some of the priority goals that came out were things near and dear to our hearts. These included a focus on Nutrition Advocates, building food literacy, and the creation of something new, which would prove to be the next stage of the Foodbank's programmatic evolution.

Welcome to the Neighborhood

The Food Action Plan became
a novel forum to build interest
around exactly the kind of
community-engaged initiatives
that the Foodbank had been
steadily working to develop, all
the way back to when we came
up with the very first Kids'
Farmers Market and insisted it
had to be taught by someone
from the community.

**FOODBANK HEALTHY
NEIGHBORHOODS**

Even before the Food Action
Plan, we had begun to engage
with a concept that I felt could be very helpful in this new work:
Asset-Based Community Development, or ABCD, for you acronym
lovers.

Traditional community development takes a "top down" approach,
where spending many millions too broadly can result in a situation
where things are worse at the end of the project than when it began.
The work of TAP (The Atlanta Project), born out of Jimmy Carter's
desire to eliminate poverty and revitalize Atlanta prior to the 1996
Olympic Games, is a well-documented example of the challenges
of community development. Its top down approach did not pay
enough attention to community voices and, as a result, many long-
term residents were ultimately displaced by the development.

Traditional community development has a habit of focusing on
deficiencies and problems, creating a negative mental map and
ensuring that resources go to existing social service agencies. There
is no encouragement of local leadership. It takes an "outside-in"

approach. ABCD creates a more optimistic mental map focusing on the capacities, dreams, and strengths of the community and is designed to build local connections and leadership. You could say it takes an "inside-out" approach.

In the old way, the deficiencies define the entire situation with problems becoming discrete units, not interlocking pieces. People become clients and programs target individual needs, not those of the community. Such a system sends the message that solutions come from outside and continues a cycle of dependency. ABCD, however, can be better sustained without large-scale funding because it works with what is already there. Issues and solutions are defined holistically as they are experienced.

The process of ABCD starts with a mapping of the community's assets and the development of a vision of the common good, in which multiple pathways are created for leadership and focus areas. Individuals mobilize and contribute their talents.

Large whole-community ABCD projects are not within the operational scope of the Foodbank (except as a partner in a broader initiative), but that has not stopped us from trying to utilize this philosophy to undergird our actions. It allows us to use food to build the groundwork of community activity, which can then morph into something that has nothing to do with nutritional health, just like we are doing with our Nutrition Advocates. We want people to be healthy and engaged in their communities. We aren't willing to be satisfied with anything less than this for the people we work with.

We thought that a good place to start to deepen this kind of work was in the City of Lompoc, a major area of poverty in Santa Barbara County. Three years back we initiated a local impact group that sought input from a wide spectrum of local people, including my daughter Lili, who was an advocate for local high schoolers. Individual neighborhood solutions were identified as a key benefit.

This resulted in the creation of a Community Food Access Center. This is a place where people can drop in to receive food, education, and support. It unites multiple educational, nutritional and community development functions. It was inspired by the work of The Stop, in Toronto, Canada. The Stop was initially a single center, but has now morphed into a non-profit that advises organizations across Canada about taking such an approach. It is a place to finally break down the barriers that prevent people gaining food literacy. We didn't have the funds to build a physical location for this center, so, with the help of a Foodbank Trustee, Tim Harrington, we were able to identify a largely disused adult education center and partnered with the school district to make use of it. Because Community Food Access Center is not exactly a warm and cuddly name to draw you in, we again turned to the community for input, and the center (in a largely Latino neighborhood) was christened Alma Cena Sana (Healthy Soul Kitchen).

Initially, the Lompoc site operates one day a week, but is intensive. Food and age-appropriate education are provided for the family at the time convenient to most. There are always activities like Zumba and my favorite: chair yoga. Helping to run the center is Sonia Sandoval, originally one of our Nutrition Advocates, and now a

ALMA CENA SANA
COMMUNITY FOOD CENTER

Learn Together
Cook Together
Eat Together
Be healthy!

FOODBANK
SANTA BARBARA COUNTY

Aprendamos Juntos
Cocinemos Juntos
Comamos Juntos
Seamos Saludables!

HOY!   *TODAY!*

leader and employee of the Foodbank. Sonia helps to inspire her peers and works with the local community. Our hope is to develop a small food business incubator to encourage entry into the local food economy by providing business, food safety, and marketing training to Nutrition Advocates and food entrepreneurs.

Collective impact projects come and go. Funding comes and goes. The idea here is to find a low-risk approach because it involves empowering the community to help itself. Networks and relationships will grow, increasing community cohesiveness and requiring less outside stimulus.

Ultimately, a neighborhood approach does not rely on the desire to help "others" but on the practical need to help "each other," by living in a neighborhood where mutual support to achieve and maintain good health reframes how people engage with each other. This can be incredibly challenging to large organizations with their "big" way of operating, but it is also exciting, representing the opportunity for a much more inclusive and empowering approach to our work, and is a signpost to the future.

Sonia Sandoval, organizer of the Lompoc Nutrition Advocates and Virginia, an advocate.

Sidebar: The Silver Tsunami

The number of senior citizens who need help from the Foodbank is exploding. People are living longer and having to survive on smaller amounts of money. Recently I got back in touch with Raquel Vela, a lady I first met a couple of years ago, when we shared a few laughs while we were waiting in line for food at one of the Foodbank's local Mobile Food Pantries, when I was doing one of my "Month on Food Stamps" challenges.

Raquel came to Santa Barbara in 1965 and is now in her 80s. She has a long history as a local volunteer in schools, and in fact was named a Santa Barbara "Local Hero" by the *Independent* newspaper back in 1996. She even walked with Cesar Chavez in the 60s. From her tiny apartment on the west side of Santa Barbara, she is still helping other families around her. Yet Raquel has to live on about $900 per month. With increased prescription charges, she struggles to keep enough healthy food on the table. Our programs have become quite literally a life saver for her, and she shared with me some of her tips for utilizing the fresh produce, protein, and dry goods items she gets from the Foodbank. She also grows zucchini, chilies, and tomatoes on a tiny patch of grass smaller than the average widescreen TV.

Over the next few years, the Foodbank and our 300 non-profit partner agencies are going to have to do more to help Raquel and the thousands like her in Santa Barbara County. Many people in their late 50s or early 60s are already struggling because employers often do not want to invest in training for those too near to retirement age.

I'm excited because Foodbank introduced a new program,

Senior Farmer's Market, which brought our national award-winning Kids Farmer's Market approach to low-income seniors living in mobile home parks. The plan is to add health screenings and other services to the fresh produce that will keep seniors healthy and able to enjoy life. We owe it to local heroes like Raquel to make sure we provide the help that seniors need.

Local Hero Raquel Vela, having to do more with less.

The Future Beckons

The last ten years have been a time of continual transformation. We started off as an efficient and dedicated organization with a narrow focus on bringing in food, storing it safely, and getting it out again. We still excel at that, but now we have become so much more, creating long-term opportunities for education and transformation for many people in our community.

So, what's next? Do we pretend that our evolution is finished? Of course not.

The next stage of evolution for our organization can be found in the slogan:

EDUCATION FOR ALL, FOOD FOR ALL WHO NEED IT.

We are proposing another pivot whereby the Foodbank becomes the recognized hub of food access, food literacy, and general nutritional health knowledge for the County of Santa Barbara. To make the maximum improvement in the health of our service area, we want to offer educational help to everyone in it. Over the last few years, we have used the *"How can we be healthy using food?"* conversation to break down all kind of barriers between "clients," "volunteers" and "donors," so the logical conclusion is that we will keep asking this question, but seek the answers within the entire community.

FOODBANK

SANTA BARBARA COUNTY

35 YEARS

FROM HUNGER INTO HEALTH

www.foodbanksbc.org

"Wait, wait, wait!" you urge. Food banks are there to provide free food to the needy. That's the reason I support you. If people have the self-motivation to be healthy, then it's great but that's their own responsibility.

I would respond to that with an emphatic YES. (Though I wouldn't use the word "needy." I can't abide the way that word is thrown around. I am definitely "needy" and everyone else I have met in the world is "needy," so needy people are not some separate, inferior group of people). Our Foodbank will never cease laboring to ensure that every food insecure person in Santa Barbara County will have enough healthy food to eat and the skills to make use of that food. We will also restrict the use of every penny that people donate to support that goal to only maintaining and improving our food services, because that is the bedrock. That is our leverage, with individuals, with our 300 member agencies, with the community.

But we can't deny that food is an agent of personal transformation. There are many Foodbank donors and volunteers who are not so focused on traditional hunger relief. They are more interested in how people can be healthy. It is to those supporters that we will look to provide separate funds for the expansion of our educational efforts.

With this new approach, we will encourage you so that if you want to find out about food and how to be healthy with it, or if you want to share your skills in this area, you go to the Foodbank. If you need food or want to give food, you go to the Foodbank. In another ten years from now, I want that to be the automatic response of a large section of the general public when asked about their perceptions of what our Foodbank is and does.

The vision statement is this: *We will use food as a tool to build lasting community connection and involvement, making Santa Barbara County nationally recognized as a landmark community where food not only builds health, but builds bridges between people.*

I get goosebumps when I read that. It is something that is truly worth doing and it can be achieved by engaging the community as a whole and using the Foodbank as the tool to achieve those goals.

As a practical road map, we will begin by expanding our national award-winning children's educational programming. I can't tell you how many times I have had parents come up to me and say that "my child learns nothing about nutrition or food in school." We want to integrate more effectively with local schools to provide this kind of education within the school day, not just in the afterschool space. We also see this education as having a powerful online component with courses and short food literacy education videos. The idea is that we will provide both online and in-person cooking and food skills training for kids, families, and others. If you can pay, you pay. If you can't, your training is free. If you want to pay it forward, then you sponsor others as well as your family. Each interaction would contain a service element and some general education about the local food system as a whole.

This will take time. Groundwork is required to build knowledge and receptivity to the Foodbank's expanded role in the food life of the community. We have already built the trust of people — supporters, volunteers, local infrastructure and services — and that is something we can use as a powerful springboard. We have a new board chair, Vibeke Staal Weiland, who is a nutritional consultant and feels passionately about the benefits of this direction, as well a new, expanded board structure, ready to rise to the challenge. We have strong new additions to our Leadership Team: Paul Wilkins, Director of Operations, comes from a farming background and was co-founder of a vineyard; Dan Thomas, our new Chief Development Officer was Chief Operating Officer, of Twin Cities

Public Television and Executive Director of Free Arts Minnesota; Lee Sherman our Director of Community Impact, came up through our development department as a Grants Manager.

It is my sincere belief that this approach will evolve the Foodbank into a self-sustaining force for health in the community. We will have moved beyond a narrow discussion about those who have enough healthy food and those who don't. Enough food will be a basic plank of the kind of community we want to be members of. We will have progressed beyond a limited view of who should encourage and guide people to be healthy with food, because that conversation is now open for all to participate in.

We will have moved from Hunger to Health.

Afterword: The Thomas Disasters — The Future is Always Messy

Carpinteria during the Thomas Fire. (Credit: Mike Eliason/SB Co. Fire Dept.)

If you march toward a future that beckons so brightly, the likelihood is that the present will throw an obstacle in your path with a mocking laugh. In our case, the obstacle had a name: Thomas.

The Thomas Fire began on December 4th, 2017, in Ventura, the county to the south of Santa Barbara. In that first terrible night, five hundred residences were destroyed, including the home of one of our board members. The fire quickly threatened the City of Ventura itself.

At first, our major challenge was serving significant numbers of people who had left homes in Ventura and were coming to Santa Barbara, and who had nutritional needs. Then, as the days went

The view from downtown Santa Barbara on the day we were evacuated.

by, the flames moved closer and closer to us, turning skies black and sending air quality spiraling into the red. This made it very unhealthy to be outside without a mask.

We had to act quickly, because many of our member agencies were not operating regular food distributions because of the poor air quality. They did not want to put their workforces in danger. It fell to senior Foodbank staff members and a host of community volunteers to put on extra indoor distributions in key areas. Foodbank CFO Carrie Wanek organized a food distribution to take place out of the Coffee Bean & Tea Leaf in her badly affected hometown of Carpinteria.

We were discovering that the fire was having a serious effect on the most economically vulnerable members of the community. No one was going to restaurants or stores. Consequently, the people who worked there were having their hours cut to the bone. Their living costs remained the same and so nutritious food was the first thing to get cut in the family budget. We increased distributions across the cities of Santa Barbara and Carpinteria.

The fire alternately crawled and leapt closer to Santa Barbara. Life became a routine of wearing a mask and living in an environment where, if you squinted, you could pretend that the light grey ash that coated everything was snow. My-six year-old daughter, Mia, was

Mia hanging up the respirators on the old Christmas tree.

looking forward to Christmas, and we had just decorated the tree when we were forced to evacuate from our house on Santa Barbara's east side for over a week. Mia and my wife, Mari, took off for the better air of Utah.

We all finally made it home for Christmas. Mia got the American Girl doll she wanted, thanks to her older sister Lili, and life returned to a shell-shocked version of normal. We had no idea that in terms of lives lost, the fire was just the beginning.

In early January, we were warned that a major rainfall was coming, which could create a mudslide from the burned hills above Montecito and Carpinteria. Some areas had mandatory evacuation orders while other areas were categorized as voluntary evacuation zones. Early on the morning of January 9th, 2018, those kinds of distinctions didn't matter.

Over half an inch of rain fell on the burned hill slopes in just five minutes. This led to rapid erosion and an incredible debris flow of mud, giant boulders, and whatever else was collected on the way down. Foodbank board member George Bean describes hearing something akin to a "thunder rumble that wouldn't

The Talkin family was lucky to spend Christmas safe in their own home.

The chapel of the Casa de Maria retreat center.

end," as the flow ripped through Montecito. That 23 would lose their lives that night and 130 homes be destroyed and over 300 homes damaged still seems like a bad dream that none of us have really woken from yet.

The economic dislocation caused by the fire turned into more of a stranglehold in the aftermath of the closing of the 101 freeway. Because Santa Barbara is wedged between mountains and the sea, if the 101 is closed, no one is going anywhere. If Mia wanted to go to her school in Carpinteria, that would require a five hour car journey (each way) around the mountains.

Eventually train service was restored, so people could sometimes get back and forth to their jobs, but with no road, Carpinteria was cut off for food resupply from our Santa Barbara warehouse. Fortunately, as members of the Feeding America network, we were able to call on Food Share, our sister food bank in Ventura County to undertake the resupply process and ensure that our member agencies in Carpinteria kept enough healthy food entering the community.

Long after the mud has dried, we continue to deal with the ongoing economic effects of the disaster in terms of many people's lost jobs and lost hours. It will take up to 18 months for those working lower-wage jobs to be able to find some kind of economic stability. We have also remained alert to the clear and present danger of future debris flows by expanding our disaster training.

Some positive things did emerge from the sorrow of these events. One was how well members of the community functioned to support each other. Another was a new community appreciation that the Foodbank is there for everyone in times of disaster, not just those at the lower end of the economic ladder. We fed rich and poor alike. There is greater awareness now that we serve as the sole delivery point for all USDA food aid coming into the area, as well as food sent by our 200 partner Feeding America regional food banks.

Will this disaster slow down our pivot toward the future? Or will it create yet another new awareness of what a food bank can be, and so allow us space to grow into the exciting new future we have planned?

Only the next ten years will tell, but I know which way I'm betting.

Mia Regina Talkin - for 6 years hard fundraising, we salute you!

EDUCATIONAL NOTES

How to Move your Organization into the Future

Like us at the Foodbank, you may reach the conclusion that you need to change what you are doing because the world around you is changing. You might have to start doing the work that really needs to be done as opposed to what you feel comfortable doing. (This is the pivot I referred to in the *Interesting Times* chapter). To help with this process, I can offer some general lessons from my experience with the Foodbank.

STEP INTO THE HELICOPTER – Take a 10,000 foot view of what you are doing and how it fits in with what else is being done by whom in this area. Your survey of activity should take a hard look at your true impact against the total need both from the perspective of the individuals you serve and the overall community needs. Consider extensive stakeholder and user interviews. You will probably find that your end users have a different perspective of your services than you do.

This was exemplified in our own situation, where an old model of food distribution (poor kids go to a room and pick up their bag of food while everyone watches) was replaced by a mutually supportive healthcare model (Healthy School Pantry) that engaged the whole family in the excitement of helping each other stay healthy with food.

WHAT IS YOUR DESTINATION? – Don't only think in terms of your existing mission, which may be too open ended or vague. Perhaps consider what "destination" you need to arrive at? (A community where...)

With our previous approach, everything was about the short term and today's crisis. Our clients are needy, and we are needy as an organization. *Help! Help!* That will get you sympathy money. That will get you "go away" money. But it will not get you the money you need to try to really solve the problem.

Look at how you can move out of your historical comfort zone and build the partnerships that will help you reach the destination in collaboration with others.

HOW CAN THE WIDER WORLD ASSIST YOUR PIVOT? – Your pivot will fail if societal and local circumstances are not in favor of it (for the Foodbank, it was donor and client interest in healthy food available for all, and also foundation interest in moving from outputs to long term outcomes). Another reason to pivot may be to avoid a big bad twister of a change in the outside world that is coming toward you.

PRETEND YOUR PIVOT IS NOT A PIVOT AT ALL – It may be easier to sell your pivot as an "evolution" as opposed to a sudden turn. It will cause less unease for all parties. And with some people, you just have to pretend nothing's changed!

DATA IS YOUR FRIEND – Use data to win the argument for your pivot. This is an excellent way of avoiding a battle of personalities. Who are the supporters who can help you compile and interpret this data?

IDENTIFY KEY INFLUENCERS – Who are the key influencers that can help you make the case for your pivot? Look for individual champions on your board, and among your volunteers and funding community, to influence others. Balance when to ask permission and when to ask for forgiveness.

PUT TOGETHER AN INTERNAL START-UP TEAM – You may have to operate like an internal start-up within your larger organization. This will be a core group of believers who can steer change.

MONEY CHANGES EVERYTHING – Money greases the most painfully grinding of wheels. Find a source of outside funding that will enable you to research or take on some small initial facet of your pivot. Use this outside money to speed internal change. This will become a win to demonstrate to those who are on the fence that your pivot will draw new forms of support.

LEARN TO LIVE WITH TWO FACES – Make peace with the fact that your pivot may require you to be a "two-faced" organization for a period of time, presenting either the old or evolved mission in different ways to different people.

It will take time, education and persuasion for donors supporting your original mission to come to understand and embrace your new mission. (What is that verse...*For what shall it nonprofit a man to gain the whole world and lose... his funding.*) When I am talking to donors, I know within 30 seconds whether I should be having a hunger or a nutrition conversation.

YOUR ORGANIZATION'S INTERNAL CULTURE CAN EAT YOUR PIVOT FOR BREAKFAST – Finally, it's not all about the outside world. Pivoting the mission is a lot easier than pivoting the culture. What is your plan for making this kind of shift internally? Identifying and empowering champions is one way. Firing, or as I say, "freeing up the future" of people who cannot move on in their thinking is another uncomfortable but vital tool. The culture is going to be the last thing to change and it will take years (culture eats mission for breakfast).

Change is a cycle. Sometimes you will be able to move faster than at others, but if your organization is not evolving at all, then it is stagnating.

How to Develop the Leadership to Make it Happen

Hamlet was always my favorite play, and it features the counselor Polonius giving endless wise advice (until he meets his unfortunate end). My dad was also a Polonius type, writing me long letters full of generalized advice while I was at college. Consequently, I have tried to go easy on the heavy handed advice to both children and staff. But I have found it useful to provide the below set of notes to staff who are emerging leaders within the organization, to encourage them to make great things happen.

1. We're not really interested in telling you what to do. We have more effective things to do with our time. We want you to be coming forward with your thought-through ideas about how to move the organization forward towards achieving our mission. How will your plan help us achieve the goals in our strategic plan? We want to say yes to your every suggestion, you just have to help us make that possible.

2. You need to be able to communicate successfully in all media to be able to sell your ideas, both internally and externally. That means you might need to pitch the same idea differently in different parts of our service area, or differently to internal or external stakeholders. You need to be more aware of their listening than you are of your own speaking.

3. The desire for continuous improvement has to be in your blood, because "good enough" is never good enough. You have to be curious about what innovations and best practices are out there, locally and nationally, both from those doing similar things to you, and others doing completely different things.

4. You have to be a coalition builder, able to step outside your day-to-day contacts to identify those stakeholders in the community who can invigorate what we are doing. We know this is hard work and that it's easier to do everything yourself, but you can't really solve things this way. Find out who out there has shared interests and objectives. Could we give up a little of our power or self-importance to partner in a meaningful way?

5. It doesn't matter whether you are in the development department or not, a large part of your job is resource acquisition for our organization. Money, people, food, services – it is all out there, and you are coming into contact with it every day. Be mindful of tapping into it and directing it through the organization. You're doing the person a favor by introducing them to our wonderful work.

6. You have to be able to inspire and lead all different kinds of people. Not just staff members, but community volunteers, interns, those who are much younger or older than you. This is a different kind of leadership from the old top down stuff.

7. Find your mentors wherever you can, inside the organization and without. There are people who will be inspired by your energy and ideas, and will want to advise you how best to make them work. Someone who is telling you all the time how things can't be done is not a mentor. Someone prepared to take a stand for your excellence is a mentor.

8. We believe our mission demands a certain urgency in its execution. That doesn't mean that it isn't possible for you to have an obscene amount of fun with large parts of your "job."

How to Pay for New Initiatives

A number of powerful trends have coalesced, resulting in a significant change in how you interact with and obtain the support of funders.

Trend #1 - Major foundations and donors are looking to invest in agencies that are actually succeeding at solving the social problem that they were set up to respond to.

Trend #2 – Major funders and foundations are becoming dissatisfied with the proliferating glut of non-profit organizations, and the duplication and inefficiencies that this brings.

You have got to come to terms with this new environment, to show that you can collaborate, evaluate, and demonstrate the outcomes of your interactions with those you serve.

Many non-profits do not want to change because of the risk of losing their existing support.

It's a numbers game. Seventy percent of your existing supporters may be locked into older perceptions of the work you are doing. Realistically, you should keep utilizing the "old" message with them, and ensure that you maintain their support.

This calculation still assumes that 30% of your supporters will be open to something new. This 30% is a beautiful flower you must nurture and grow. These supporters are typically younger, more interested in getting directly involved, and want campaigns with end results that they can feel good about achieving.

As you begin to think through your new approaches, don't feel you have to have everything figured out before you take it to supporters.

They want to be co-creators with you. Consider having visioning lunches or events that could bring in a third party expert/speaker to validate your new approach. Consider program tours that take your supporters to programs run by other organizations that you want to emulate. You needn't be afraid that they'll jump ship. If you have the relationship with the donor, they will appreciate you being honest that you don't have all the answers and will be excited about the possibility of learning from success elsewhere.

FIND NOVEL PARTNERS

As your aspirations to do new things become known in the community, you have the opportunity to build novel partnerships that will enhance your legitimacy about venturing into a broader perspective of how your work builds the resiliency of the community.

These novel partnerships are going to excite funders because they are a more realistic response to the total picture that they see out there, rather than one organization doing the same thing endlessly with no clear improvement in the overall situation.

You will get your fingers burned with some partnerships, where some groups might not want you "invading" their area, so it is important to have limited objectives that allow trust and true partnership to grow over a period of time.

Expanding and deepening your donor base does not require a shift in mission, but a broader expression of an organization's identity/profile and a fluid and responsive advancement of your mission.

And it's not just how your organization presents itself to the outside world. You need to question the assignment and evaluation of fundraising staff members as nothing more than donation solicitors.

That's a change of mindset for many of us. We want to keep pouring the pressure on the fundraisers to live or die by last quarter's figures, but successful fundraising has become far more demanding and complex than simply preparing for and conducting requests for philanthropic contributions.

We need to *advance* and *support* an understanding and assignment of fundraising staff members as being:

- **Relationship/partnership builders (internal & external)**
- **Project managers**
- **Program development partners**
- **Conveners**
- **Deal-makers**
- **Translators**

The goal is to emphasize OUTCOMES rather than OUTPUTS. More than ever, foundations are seeking new systemic, sustainable, and scalable strategies and solutions to persistent problems.

Here's a thought-provoking "Golden Rule" for Expanding Philanthropic Support, that I got from Wally Verdooren, past Director of Strategic Grant Making at Feeding America and now Development Director at Roadrunner Food Bank in New Mexico:

"Whatever you're buying, we're selling."

While that might initially sound like desperation or the first symptoms of mission drift, what Wally is really suggesting is that you focus FIRST on the donor's/prospect's motivations and goals for giving and not on giving towards your organization's needs, interests, and programs.

You should also go long and go deep in your prospective funder search by assessing motivations and goals for giving generally and specifically and then aligning them with what your organization actually does. This requires not only knowing your organization well, but not letting others define it.

CONSIDER THE FUNDER PERSPECTIVE

The day to day reality of the funder can be a state of overwhelm from the sheer number of inquiries and applications for resources. The dilemma is that many programs deserve support. One way that you can break from the hungry pack is to demonstrate that your initiative is strength-based versus deficit-based. The former are positive, community-driven efforts that go behind the behavior to look at the drivers of that behavior. Deficit-based efforts just respond to the behavior. Research has shown that strength-based interventions are sustainable, whereas deficit-based activities are ineffective and may make the situation worse.

If your new direction is worthwhile and well thought out, the money to fund it is out there. Good luck!

Erik and Mari Talkin attending our fundraising event: Fork and Cork Classic.

RESOURCES

ORGANIZATIONS
Foodbank of Santa Barbara County, www.foodbanksbc.org
Hunger into Health Blog, www.hungerintohealth.com
SB County Food Action Plan, www.sbcfoodaction.org
Feeding America, www.feedingamerica.org
Closing the Hunger Gap, www.thehungergap.org
California Association of Foodbanks, www.cafoodbanks.org
Jeff Bridges End Hunger Network, www.jeffbridges.com/endhunger
Share Our Strength, www.nokidhungry.org
The Stop, www.thestop.org
Orfalea Foundation, www.orfaleafoundation.org
Santa Barbara Foundation, www.sbfoundation.org
Weingart Foundation, www.weingartfnd.org
Hutton Parker Foundation, www.huttonfoundation.org
Mccune Foundation, www.mccunefoundation.org

BOOKS
Adler, David A. *The Life and Cuisine of Elvis Presley* Three Rivers Press, 1993.

Kelly, Colleen and Lynda Gerty. *The Abundant Not-For-Profit: How talent (not money) will transform your organization* Vantage Point, 2013.

Kretzmann, John P. and John L. McKnight. *Building Communities from the Inside Out: A Path toward Finding and Mobilizing a Community's Assets* ACTA Publications, 1993.

Lupton, Robert. *Toxic Charity: How Churches and Charities Hurt Those They Help (And How To Reverse It)* HarperOne, 2011.

Poppendieck, Janet. *Sweet Charity? Emergency Food and the End of Entitlement.* Penguin Random House, 1999.

Made in the USA
Columbia, SC
19 February 2019